BROWERE'S LIFE MASKS
OF GREAT AMERICANS

LECTOR HOUSE PUBLIC DOMAIN WORKS

BROWERE'S LIFE MASKS OF GREAT AMERICANS

CHARLES HENRY HART

ǀ

ISBN: 978-93-5614-189-6

Published: -

LECTOR HOUSE LLP
E-MAIL: lectorpublishing@gmail.com

THOMAS JEFFERSON

Age 82

BROWERE'S LIFE MASKS
OF GREAT AMERICANS

BY

CHARLES HENRY HART

TO
THE MEMORY OF
JAMES P. SMITH
MINIATURE PAINTER
WHO FIRST DEVELOPED MY TASTE FOR ART
I INSCRIBE THIS VOLUME AS A
TOKEN OF GRATITUDE

PROEM

"G"REAT oaks from little acorns grow." How big results may flow from small beginnings is typically illustrated by the possibilities of the present volume. It began with the bare knowledge that there was, once upon a time, a man by the name of Browere, who had some facility in making masks from the living face. This was the seed that was destined to expand into the present publication. To tell how this germ grew, would be to anticipate the recital in the following pages; but the lively interest shown by the wide public and by the narrow public, the people and the artistic circle, in the articles upon Browere's Life Masks of Great Americans, contributed by the writer to "McClure's Magazine," has called for a more expanded history of the artist and his work, for which fortunately there is ample material.

To the grandchildren of Browere, who have reverently preserved the works of their ingenious ancestor and generously placed them at my disposal for reproduction, are due the heartiest thanks; and in view of the possibility of the dispersal of the collection, it should be secured, *en bloc*, by the Government of the United States, and the most important of the life masks cast in imperishable bronze.

CHARLES HENRY HART.

Philadelphia, October 1, 1898.

CONTENTS

LIST OF PLATES

LIFE MASKS

I

THE PLASTIC ART

THE plastic art, which is the art of modelling in the round with a pliable material, was with little doubt the earliest development of the imitative arts. To an untrained mind it is a more obvious method, of copying or delineating an object, than by lines on a flat surface. Its origin is so early and so involved in myths and legends, that any attempt to ascribe its invention, to a particular nation or to a particular individual, is impossible. Its earliest form was doubtless monumental. Frequent passages in the Scriptures show this, and that the Hebrews practised it, as did also their neighbors the Phœnicians; while excavations have revealed the early plastic monuments of the Assyrians. For more than two thousand years the Egyptians are known to have associated the plastic arts with their religious worship, but, being bound within priestly rules, made no perceptible progress from its beginning; yet these crude monuments of ancient Egypt are now the records of the world's history of their time.

Associated with architecture from its earliest development, it has, in its narrower form of sculpture, been called, not inaptly, "the daughter of architecture." Indeed, in the remains of ancient monuments, the two arts are so intimately combined, that architecture is frequently subordinated to sculpture, particularly in the buildings of the middle ages, where they appear as very twin sisters, sculpture often supplying structural parts of the erection.

Among the Greeks the plastic art existed from time immemorial, and among them attained its highest proficiency and skill. That they exceeded all others in this art goes without saying; their familiarity with the human form enabling them to portray corporal beauty with a delicacy and perfection, that no society, reared in any other situation or surrounded by other influences, could ever attain. With them beauty was the chief aim, it having in their eyes so great a value that everything was subservient to it. As has been said, "It was above law, morality, modesty, and justice." Greek art, as we know it, began about 600 B.C.; but it did not arrive at its perfection until the time of Pericles, a century and a half later, in the person of Pheidias, who consummately illustrates its most striking characteristics—the simplicity with which great efforts are attained, and the perfect harmony which obtains between the desire and the conception, the realization and the execution.

The frieze of the Parthenon, which easily holds the supreme place among known works of sculpture, is ample proof of this.

It was a Greek of the time of Alexander the Great, in the century following that of Pheidias, who invented the art of taking casts from the human form. This honor, according to Pliny, belongs to Lysistratus, a near relative of the famous sculptor Lysippus, who made life casts with such infinite skill as to produce strikingly accurate resemblances. The art of making life casts did not, however, come into general use until the middle of the fifteenth century, when Andrea Verocchio, the most noted pupil of Donatello, and the instructor of Perugini and of Leonardo da Vinci, followed it with such success as to lead Vasari, Bottari, and others to ascribe to him its invention. It was this art of taking casts from the human form, so successfully followed in this country, nearly four hundred years later, by John Henri Isaac Browere, that has afforded the occasion for the present work.

II

THE PLASTIC ART IN AMERICA

EFORE entering upon the subject of Browere and his life masks, it seems proper, if not actually necessary, to take a survey of the development of the plastic art in that part of America now embraced within the limits of the United States, prior to the time of Browere, so as to understand what influences may have been exerted upon him in the direction of his career. This becomes the more important from the fact that while there have appeared in print, from time to time, numerous references to this subject, not a single consideration of the topic, known to the writer, has presented the facts with that accuracy without which all deductions must be in vain. From the present consideration the plastic work of the aborigines is necessarily excluded, as it belongs to another and very different department of study; this having to do with a branch of the fine arts, and that with a phase of archæology.

Prior to the war of the Revolution, while there were among us several painters exercising their art, both those of foreign and those of native birth, no note has come down of any modeller or sculptor in our midst, save one—a very remarkable woman named Patience Wright. It may be that we had no need for the sculptor's art. We were mere colonies without call for statues or for monuments. It is true there was the leaden figure of King George, on the Bowling Green, in New York; but it came from the mother country, and soon furnished bullets for her rebellious sons. Likewise came from across the ocean the odd bits of decoration intended as architectural aids in the building of old Christ Church, in Philadelphia, and of a few other noted buildings. But our first practitioner of the plastic art was, as has been said, a woman.

Patience Lovell was born in Bordentown, New Jersey, of Quaker parentage, in 1725, and died in London, March 23, 1786. When twenty-three she married Joseph Wright, who, twenty-one years later, left her a widow with three children. She had early shown her aptitude for modelling, using dough, putty, or any other material that came in her way; and, being left by her husband unprovided for, she made herself known by her small portraits in wax, chiefly profile bas-reliefs. In 1772, she sought a wider field for her abilities by removing to London, where for many years she was the rage, not only for her plastic work, but for her extraordinary conversational powers, which drew to her all the political and social leaders of the day. By this means she was kept fully advised as to the momentous events transpiring relative to the colonies; and being on terms of familiar intercourse with Doctor Franklin (whose profile she admirably modelled, it being afterward reproduced by Wedgwood), she communicated her information regularly to him, as shown by her numerous letters preserved in his manuscript correspondence.

Mrs. Wright had a piercing eye, which seems to have penetrated to the very soul of her sitters, and enabled her to read their inner-selves and fix their characters in their features. Of her three children, one daughter married John Hoppner, the eminent portrait-painter; another, Elizabeth Pratt, followed her mother's profession of modelling small portraits in wax; and the son, Joseph, we shall have occasion to mention on a subsequent page. Some idea may be gathered of the meritorious quality of Mrs. Wright's work from the fact that she modelled in wax a whole-length statue of the great Chatham, which, protected in a glass case, was honored with a place in Westminster Abbey. Although Patience Wright never aspired to what is recognized as high art, still her abilities were of a high order, and her career is a most interesting one to follow and reflect upon, as she was the first native American, of American parentage, to follow the art of modelling as a profession. Her knowledge must have been wholly self-acquired, and in an environment not conducive to the development of an artistic temperament.

Mrs. Wright is not known to have essayed sculpture, or to have worked in any resisting material, so that the first native American sculptor was William Rush. He was born in Philadelphia, July 4, 1756, being fourth in direct descent from John Rush, who commanded a troop of horse in Cromwell's army, and, having embraced the principles of the Quakers, came to Pennsylvania the year following the landing of William Penn. From the emigrant John Rush was also descended, in the fifth generation, the celebrated Benjamin Rush, physician and politician, and one of the signers of the Declaration of Independence. The father of William was Joseph Rush, who married, at Christ Church, Philadelphia, September 19, 1750, Rebecca Lincoln, daughter of Abraham Lincoln, of Springfield Township, now in Delaware County, Pennsylvania. She was of the same family as Abraham Lincoln, the martyr President of the United States. I am thus minute in tracing the ancestry of William Rush, in order to establish and place upon record, beyond a question or doubt, that he was the first American sculptor by birth and parentage, and thus set at rest, the claim, so frequently made, that this honor belongs to John Frazee,[1] a man not born until 1790.

Rush served in the army of the Revolution, and it was not until after peace had settled on the land that he seems to have turned his attention to art. He soon became noted for the life-like qualities he put into the figureheads, for the prows of ships, he was called upon to carve, and so noted did these works become, that many orders came to him from Britain, for figureheads for English ships. The story is told that when a famous East Indiaman, the *Ganges*, sailed up that river, to Calcutta, with a figure of a river-god, carved by Rush, at its prow, the natives clambered about it as an object of adoration and of worship. Benjamin H. Latrobe,

---

[1] "Schools and Masters of Sculpture," by A. G. Radcliffe, 1894.

the noted architect, in a discourse before the Society of Artists of the United States, in 1811, says, speaking of Rush: "His figures, forming the head or prow of a vessel, place him, in the excellence of his attitudes and actions, among the best sculptors that have existed; and in the proportion and drawing of his figures he is often far above mediocrity and seldom below it. There is a motion in his figures that is inconceivable. They seem rather to draw the ship after them than to be impelled by the vessel. Many are of exquisite beauty. I have not seen one on which there is not the stamp of genius."

Rush was a man of warm imagination and of a lively ideality. These are shown by his figures symbolical of Strength, Wisdom, Beauty, Faith, Hope, and Charity, carved by him for the Masonic Temple; by his figures of "Praise" and "Exaltation," two cherubim encircled by glory, in St. Paul's Episcopal Church; and by his "Christ on the Cross," carved for St. Augustine's Roman Catholic Church. His best-known work is his whole-length statue of Washington, carved in 1815, from recollection, by the aid of Houdon's bust, which it closely resembles, now in the old State-house, or Independence Hall, Philadelphia. Another noted work of his, from Miss Vanuxem, a celebrated Quaker City belle, having posed for the model, is the graceful figure of a nymph, with a swan, located upon a rocky perch opposite the wheel-house at Fairmount water-works, Philadelphia.

Beside carving in wood, Rush modelled in clay, and his portrait-busts have always been recognized as truthful and satisfactory likenesses. The bust most commonly seen of Lafayette is his work. William Rush died in the city of his birth on the seventeenth day of January, 1833; and considering the era in which he lived and its uncongenial atmosphere, his achievement is most noteworthy and commendable.

Twelve days after the birth of Rush, Joseph Wright came into the world, inheriting from his mother her artistic temperament. At sixteen he accompanied the family to England, and received instruction from Benjamin West and from his brother-in-law, Hoppner. He returned to America late in 1782, bringing a letter of commendation from Franklin to Washington. In 1783, he painted a portrait of Washington from life, at Rocky Hill, New Jersey, and the next year was permitted to make a cast of Washington's face, which is said to have been broken irreparably in removing from the skin,—a story the veracity of which may be akin to that in regard to Browere's mask of Jefferson, hereafter to be told. However this may be, Wright made a bust of Washington, for which Congress paid him "233⅓ dollars," and also modelled in wax a laureated profile portrait of Washington, which is of both artistic and historical value. Wright died in Philadelphia, during the yellow fever epidemic of December, 1793, and his bust, by his friend Rush, whom he is said to have instructed in clay modelling, belongs to the Academy of the Fine Arts, at Philadelphia.

Patience Wright, her son Joseph, and William Rush are the only native Americans that we know to have worked at the plastic art during the period we have limited for this review; and thus John Frazee, who claimed to be, and therefore is commonly credited with being, the first native American sculptor of American parentage, need not be considered; for he was only two years old when Browere was born, and therefore can have had no part in influencing Browere's career.

There were, however, two foreigners who certainly did exercise a decided influence upon art in America, and cannot properly be omitted from any consideration of the causes that helped the plastic art onward in these United States. Both of them were men of commanding ability and importance in sculpture. One was the eminent French statuary Houdon, who visited this country in 1785, to prepare himself to produce his famous statue of Washington; and the other, the not much less able Italian, Giuseppe Ceracchi, who came here, in 1791, for love of freedom, and lived among us about four years. Ceracchi's plan for an elaborate monument to commemorate the American Revolution, which was warmly taken up by Washington and members of the cabinet, and received the consideration of Congress, made his artistic proclivities better known, and gave the subject a wider range than the limited scope of Houdon's work. Yet the influence of both these eminent devotees of the plastic art left, without doubt, a strong impression upon the minds of the people—an impression constantly refreshed by the sight of their works, which helped to create a healthy atmosphere for the development of a taste among us for the plastic art.

NOTE. John Dixey, an Irishman about whom little is known, and John Eckstein, a German by birth and an Englishman by adoption and education, settled here toward the close of the last century, and both did some work in modelling and in stone-cutting; but they were of mediocre ability, and left no impression upon the artistic instinct of the people.

III

JOHN HENRI ISAAC BROWERE

HAT one generation fails to appreciate, and therefore decries and sneers at, a subsequent one comprehends and applauds. It is conspicuously so in discovery, in science, in poetry, and in art; so much depends upon the point of view and the environment of the observed and of the observer. Were these remarks not true, the very remarkable collection of busts from life masks, taken at the beginning of the second quarter of the present century, by John Henri Isaac Browere, almost an unknown name a year ago, would not have been hidden away until their recent unearthing. The circumstances that led to their discovery are as curious as that the busts should have been neglected and forgotten for so long.

John Henri Isaac Browere, the son of Jacob Browere and Ann Catharine Gendon, was born at No. 55, Warren Street, New York city, November 18, 1792, and died at his house opposite the old mile-stone, in the Bowery, in the city of his birth, September 10, 1834, and was buried in the Carmine Street Churchyard. He was of Dutch descent, one of those innumerable claimants of heirship to Anneke Jans, through Adam Brouwer, of Ceulen, who came to this country and settled on Long Island, in 1642. Adam Brouwer's name was really Berkhoven, but the name of his business, Brouwer or Brewer, became attached to him, so that his descendants have been transmitted by his trade-name, and thus, as is often the case, a new surname introduced. His second son, Jacob Adam Brouwer, or Jacob son of Adam the Brewer, married Annetje Bogardus, granddaughter of Reverend Edward Bogardus and Anneke Jansen (corrupted to Jans); and among the most persistent pursuers of the intangible fortune of Anneke Jans has been the family of Browere.

John Browere was entered as a student at Columbia College, but did not remain to be graduated, owing doubtless to his early marriage, on April 30, 1811, to Eliza Derrick, of London, England. He turned his attention to art and became a pupil of Archibald Robertson, the miniature-painter, who came to this country from Scotland, in 1791, with a commission from David Stuart, Earl of Buchan, to paint, for his gallery at Aberdeen, a portrait of Washington. Later on, Archibald Robertson, with his brother Alexander, opened at No. 79, Liberty Street, New York, the well-known Columbian Academy, where, for thirty years, these Scotchmen maintained a school, for the instruction of both sexes in drawing and in painting, and where Vanderlyn, Inman, Cummings, and other of the early New York artists, profited by their training. At the present time, when miniature-painting is again coming into vogue, it is interesting to reflect that the letters which passed between Archibald Robertson in this country, and his brother Andrew in Scotland, form the best treatise that can be found upon the charming art of painting in little. These letters, after having remained in manuscript for the better part of a century, have recently been given to the public, in a charming volume of "Letters and Papers of Andrew Robertson," edited by his daughter, Miss Emily Robertson, of Lansdowne Terrace, Hampton Wick, England.

JOHN HENRI ISAAC BROWERE

Determined to improve himself still further, Browere accepted the offer of his brother, who was captain of a trading-vessel to Italy, to accompany him abroad; and for nearly two years the young man travelled on foot through Italy, Austria, Greece, Switzerland, France, and England, diligently studying art and more especially sculpture. Returning to New York, he began modelling, and soon produced a bust of Alexander Hamilton, from Archibald Robertson's well-known miniature of the Federal martyr, which was pronounced a meritorious attempt to produce a model in the round from a flat surface. Being of an inventive turn, he began experimenting to obtain casts from the living face in a manner and with a composition different from those commonly employed by sculptors. After many trials and failures, he perfected his process, with the superior results shown in his work.

Browere's first satisfactory achievement was a mask of his friend and preceptor, Robertson, and his second was that of Judge Pierrepont Edwards, of Connecticut. But the most important of his very early works was the mask of John Paulding, the first to die of the captors of André; and this mask, made in 1817, was followed later by masks of Paulding's coadjutors, Williams and Van Wart; so that we owe to Browere's nimble fingers the only authentic likenesses we have of these conspicuous patriots of the Revolution.

Browere wrote verse and painted pictures in addition to his modelling, and, in the spring of 1821, made an exhibition at the old gallery of the American Academy of the Fine Arts, in Chambers Street, New York, which called forth the following card from his early instructor, Robertson, who was one of the directors of the Academy. It is interesting, notwithstanding the unconscious partiality one is apt to have for a former pupil, and is addressed:

To the American Public.

> Having for many years been intimately acquainted with John H. I. Browere, of the City of New York, I deem it a duty which I owe to him as an artist, and to the public as judges, to say that from my own observation of his works both as a painter, poet, and sculptor, I think him endowed with a great genius by nature and first talents by industry. This my opinion, his works lately exhibited in the Gallery of the American Academy of Fine Arts, New York, fully justify and is amply corroborated by all, who with unprejudiced eye, view the works of his hand.

> Archibald Robertson.

New York, May 21, 1821.

It was left, however, for "The Nation's Guest" to lift Browere's art into prominence. At the request of the New York city authorities, Lafayette permitted Browere, in July of 1825, to make a cast of his face. This was so successful that from this time on, Browere was devoted to making casts of the most noted characters in the country's history, who were then living, with the purpose of forming a national gallery of the busts of famous Americans. He intended to have them reproduced in bronze, and devoted years of labor and the expenditure of much money to the furtherance of his scheme. He wrote to Madison: "Pecuniary emolument never has been my aim. The honor of being favored by my country biases sordid views." In 1828 he wrote to the same: "I have expended $12,087 in the procuration of the specimens I now have." These included masks of Presidents John and John Quincy Adams, Jefferson, and Madison, and later was added that of Van Buren; Charles Carroll of Carrollton; Lafayette; De Witt Clinton; Generals Philip Van Cortlandt, Alexander Macomb and Jacob Brown; Commodore David Porter; Secretary of the Navy Samuel L. Southard of New Jersey; and Secretary of the Treasury Richard Rush of Pennsylvania; Justice of the United States Supreme Court Philip Pendleton Barbour; and the great commoner, Henry Clay; Doctors Samuel Latham Mitchill, Valentine Mott, and David Hosack; Edwin Forrest and Tom Hilson, the actors; Charles Francis Adams and Philip Hone; Thomas Addis Emmet and Doctor Cooper of South Carolina; Colonel Stone and Major Noah, of newspaper notoriety; Dolly Madison and Francis Wright; Gilbert Stuart, Paulding, Williams, and Van Wart; and other personages favorably known in their day, but who have slipped out of the niche of worldly immortality, so that even their names fail to awaken a recollection of themselves. Such is the mutability of fame.

The time, however, was not ripe for the public patronage of the Fine Arts. There was, too, a feeling abroad that it savored of monarchy and favored classes, to perpetuate men and deeds by statues and monuments. Another cause that hampered Browere was the lack of protection accorded to such works. He complains to Madison: "I regret to say that as yet no law has been passed to protect modelling and sculpture, and therefore I have been hindered from completing the gallery, fearful of having the collection pirated." So disheartened did he become with the little interest shown in his project and the work he had accomplished for it, that at one time he contemplated visiting Panama, and presenting the busts of the more prominent subjects to the republics of South America, in order to incite them to further efforts for freedom. Finally he was forced to abandon his scheme of a national gallery, owing to want of support, and the direct opposition — "jealous enmity," Browere calls it — of his brother artists, the old American Academy faction led by Colonel Trumbull, and the new National Academy followers led by William Dunlap.

They maligned his pretensions because he was honest enough to call his method for accomplishing what he attempted *"a process."* Surely, judging from results, it was superior to any other known method of obtaining a life mask, and it seems most unfortunate that his "process" has to be counted among "the lost arts"; for neither he nor his son, who was acquainted with both the composition and the method of applying it, has left a word of information on the subject. When the public press attacked Browere and his method for the rumored maltreatment of President Jefferson, he replied: "Mr. Browere never has followed and never will follow the usual course, knowing it to be fallacious and absolutely bad. The manner in which he executes portrait-busts from life is unknown to all but himself, and the invention is his own, for which he claims exclusive rights, but it is infinitely milder than the usual course." That his method of taking the mask was accomplished without discomfort to the subject is fully attested by the number of persons who submitted to it, as also by the many certificates given by Jefferson,

Adams, Madison, Lafayette, Gilbert Stuart, and others to that effect.

In the following letter from Browere to Trumbull it will be seen the writer does not attempt to conceal his feelings of resentment:

NEW YORK, 12 July, 1826.

Sir:

The very illiberal and ungentleman-like manner in which Col. Trumbull treated the execution, &c., of my portrait-busts of Ex-President Adams and Honorable Charles Carroll with the statue of Ex-President Jefferson, late displayed in the banquetting hall of the Hon. Common Council of New York, has evidenced a personal ill-will and hostility to me that I shall not pass over in silence. The envy and jealousy inherent in your nature and expressed in common conversations intimate to me a man of a perverse and depraved mind.

Rest assured, Sir, I fear not competition with you as a portrait or historic painter; I know your fort, and your failings. To convince you that I know somewhat of the Arts of Design, I shall immediately commence an analysis of your four pictures painted for Congress, and shall endeavor therein to refer to each and every figure plagiarized from English and other prints. Your assertion to me that you made your portraits therein to correspond with their characters, will assuredly go for as much as they deserve. In my opinion, ideal likenesses ought not to be palmed on a generous public for real ones.

Remember what was said on the floor of Congress in reference to your four celebrated pictures: "Instead of being worth $32,000 they were not worth 32 cents." In remembering this remember that "nemo me impune lacessit." And by attending to your own concerns you will retain a reputation or name of being an able artist and not a slanderer.

BROWERE, *Sculptor*.

Colonel Trumbull has endorsed this letter: "*Browere. Poor man! too much vanity hath made him mad.*"

However, from a letter written three years later to the Directors of the American Academy of the Fine Arts, and "*Favored by Col. Trumbull*," it would appear that the two artists had healed their differences; but Browere's feeling of resentment toward the National Academy of Design knew no abatement. He was kept out of the National Academy by Dunlap, who also ignored him in his malevolent and unreliable "History of the Arts of Design in the United States." The cause for this, as stated by Browere's son, was that before Browere had ever met Dunlap he was asked his opinion of Dunlap's painting of "Death on the Pale Horse," then on public exhibition. He replied: "It's a strong work, but looks as if it were painted by a man with but one eye." This remark was reported to Dunlap, who actually had but one eye. He was mortally offended at the sculptor's insight, and became his undying enemy. Browere wrote to the Academy as follows:

NEW YORK, 31 July, 1829.

Gentlemen:

For several years past I have strictly devoted myself to the profession of the liberal arts and flatter myself that my efforts have not been detrimental to their interests. The reason why or wherefore I, an American artist, bearing with me an unblemished moral reputation, should have been selected for exclusion by both the American Academy of Fine Arts, as well as the self-denominated Academy of Design, appears mysterious and illiberal, and not in accordance with the principles of religion or democracy. Had not an enthusiastic love of and devotion to the Fine Arts guided my reason, at this day I should have become one of the most inveterate enemies to both institutions. Philosophy has made me what I now am, viz., the sincere friend of man and admirer of the works of his hands. As such I have,—written injuries as sand—favors on the tablet of memory.

As one of the great body of artists of America I deem it an incumbent duty to advance the beauteous arts by all honorable means, and to chastise arrogance, presumption, ignorance, and wilful malevolence. With chagrin I have viewed the sinister and aristocratical proceedings of the National Academy, and the ill results that must eventually follow its longer continuance, and therefore have publicly deprecated its wickedness. As one of the regenerators of the old or American Academy of Fine Arts, I now make bold in saying to its directors a few things, which if duly weighed and followed must result favorably to its vitality and best interests, and be the medium of establishing the reputation of artists on firm and lasting basis, viz.: by collecting around the American Academy and with it all the genius and talent in the arts of design which our country possesses and creating a fund sufficient to all its wants and expenditures.

Already, twenty-five artists of respectability of this city await one effort of the American Academy to reëstablish its original standing and reputation, and they will join heart and hand to oppose the Academy of Design (truly so called) by every work of their hands done and to be done. The one effort alluded to is to procure at a reasonable rent say from 800 to 1000 dollars per annum the second story of the large and splendid building now erecting corner of Anthony Street and Broadway. The undersigned is perfectly well assured that from $1000 to $1500 per annum can be realized (exclusive of rent) from daily exhibitions of the works of living artists not in connection with the National

Academy. He is fully satisfied from late observations that twenty-five new pieces or paintings can be procured monthly, all of which may be procured on loan for one month at least. This being the case the Academy must eventually and in a very short time supplant the puny efforts of a few National Esquires, a majority of whom are scarce entering their teens.

The subscribing artist respectfully informs you that the exhibition of the rough specimens of his art, viz., "The Inquisition of Spain," at No. 315 Broadway, did positively realize to him, in eighteen months, *Seven thousand and sixty-nine dollars*. If, then, such an exhibition could realize such a sum, what would an exhibition of splendid historic and allegoric subjects, with portraits, miniatures, and landscapes by our native artists, not realize under the guidance of such a respectable board of directors as is that of the American Academy of Fine Arts?

The names of Trumbull, Vanderlyn, Frothingham, etc., alone would act as magic on a discriminating public, provided fair specimens of their talents be judiciously arranged for public inspection. Boston has done wonders this year in her Athenæum. Why, then, should we, equally blessed with native talent, despair, and sit down in sack-cloth and ashes, when a single effort can make us her equal and rival? Gentlemen, I am enthusiastic, and yet have maturely weighed each and every reason against your regeneration, and boldly assert more is for you than against you. The three preceding mentioned gentlemen are equal to, if not superior in talent to, any Boston can produce. Our portrait-painters generally bid fair to excel. All that is wanted is your help as a body corporate, your co-operation as lovers of the Fine Arts. Where, if you become extinct, shall we go to study the models of antiquity? Alas! we know of no other place wherein the experience of ages is collected, en masse, no place wherein to receive that instruction so essential to a knowledge of our profession. Mr. Bowen, the proprietor, has offered to you through Colonel Trumbull, the room alluded to at a fair compensation; it now rests with you to say for once and for all, "We will," or, "we will not continue the patrons of art." Wishing to yourselves individually, and collectively as a body corporate, health and peace, I remain,

Gentlemen, truly your Friend in the Fine Arts,
JOHN H. I. BROWERE.

No formal action is known to have been taken upon this communication; but the antagonism plainly evident as existing between the new Academy of Design and the old Academy of the Fine Arts, forms a lively chapter in the history of American art. Full particulars of the strife are given in Dunlap's book and in Cummings's "Historic Annals of the National Academy of Design." But these accounts are from biased adherents of the new institution and bitter opponents of the old, so that, for a brief but philosophical and judicial consideration of the subject, one must turn to John Durand's sketch of Colonel Trumbull in the "American Art Review" for 1880.

Browere died, after only a few hours' illness, of cholera; and it is pathetic to picture the disappointed sculptor, on his deathbed, directing, as he did, that the heads should be sawed off the most important busts, and boxed up for forty years, at the end of which period he hoped their exhibition would elicit recognition for their merit and value as historical portraits from life. This directed mutilation was not made; but the busts never saw the light of day until the Centennial year, when a few of them were placed on exhibition in Philadelphia. But not being connected with the national celebration, they were a mere side-show, and were not in a position to attract attention. Indeed, the fact of their exhibition was unheralded, and has only recently become known.

Call Browere's work what one will,—process, art, or mechanical,—the result gives the most faithful portrait possible, down to the minutest detail, the very living features of the breathing man, a likeness of the greatest historical significance and importance. A single glance will show the marked difference between Browere's work and the ordinary life cast by the sculptor or modeller, no matter how skilful he may be. Browere's work is real, human, lifelike, inspiring in its truthfulness, while other life masks, even the celebrated ones by Clark Mills, who made so many, are dead and heavy, almost repulsive in their lifelessness. It seems next to marvelous how he was able to preserve so wonderfully the naturalness of expression. His busts are imbued with animation; the individual character is there, so simple and direct that, next to the living man, he has preserved for us the best that we can have—a perfect *facsimile*. One experiences a satisfaction in contemplating these busts similar to that afforded by the reflected image of the daguerreotype. Both may be "inartistic" in the sense that the artist's conception is wanting; but for historical human documents they outweigh all the portraits ever limned or modelled.

Browere left a wife and eight children, his second child and eldest son, Alburtis D. O. Browere, inheriting the artistic temperament of the father. He was born at Tarrytown, March 17, 1814, and died at Catskill, February 17, 1887. After his father's death, he entered the schools of the National Academy of Design, and, in 1841, gained the first prize of $100, in competition with twenty-four others, for his picture of "Canonicus Treating with the English," as detailed in Thatcher's "Lives of the Indians." Previous to this, when only eighteen years old, he was awarded a silver medal, by the American Institute in New York, "for the best original oil painting," the title of which has been forgotten. He painted several pictures with Rip Van Winkle as the subject, and among his contemporaries and friends was highly appreciated as an artist and as a man. He went to California soon after the opening to the east of that El Dorado, where he remained several years, painting many pictures of mining scenes. It was he who added the draperies to the busts made from his father's life masks—an addition much to be regretted; but, on the other hand, it was his filial reverence that preserved these invaluable human documents, and has permitted us to see and know how many of the great characters who have gone before really appeared in the flesh, how they actually looked when they lived and moved and had their being.

IV

THE CAPTORS OF ANDRÉ

"WHILE Arnold is handed down with execration to future times, posterity will repeat with reverence the names of Van Wart, Paulding, and Williams." These words of Alexander Hamilton, written to John Laurens shortly after the taking of André, form a fitting text for the chapter introducing Browere's busts of those patriots. It is fitting, because of the varying winds that have blown over the subject, swaying public opinion first one way and then the other; until finally the full prophecy of Hamilton is accepted as the right judgment of posterity. Of course, my comments refer only to the captors of André; there never has been but one judgment as to the execrated Arnold.

It required more than a generation for any voice to let itself be heard questioning the sincerity and patriotism of the three lads who brought André to justice. And then it was the voice of only one man, Colonel Tallmadge, who had come under André's winsome fascinations, while acting as officer of the guard over the unfortunate spy from his capture to his execution. The occasion for the unworthy onslaught of Tallmadge, was a resolution offered in the House of Representatives, at Washington, to increase the beggarly pension of $200 per annum, awarded, with a silver medal, by the Continental Congress, to each of the three,—Paulding, Williams, and Van Wart. Tallmadge opposed it, not upon the ground that these men had not done the deed history accords to them and thereby possibly saved the new nation, but because André, the captured spy, while in captivity, had told his keeper that they deceived him into believing they were British soldiers, and when he found they were not, but were American militiamen and he their prisoner, he could have bought his freedom if he had been weighted down with gold. Suppose this story of André, as retailed by Tallmadge, thirty-seven years after the happening of the event, is accepted at its fullest value—what does it signify? At best it is a mere surmise, hardly even the expression of an opinion; and that it was baseless is shown most emphatically by the express denial of each one of the captors, under oath, when Tallmadge made his ill-judged and unpatriotic charge. British gold was ever present during the Revolution to debauch patriots and make them traitors, acting upon the doctrine of Sir Robert Walpole, that every man has his price; therefore André surmised that three ragged, unpaid, militiamen would easily have yielded could they have seen the yellow glitter; but subsequent events clearly disprove that the prisoner could have bought his freedom.

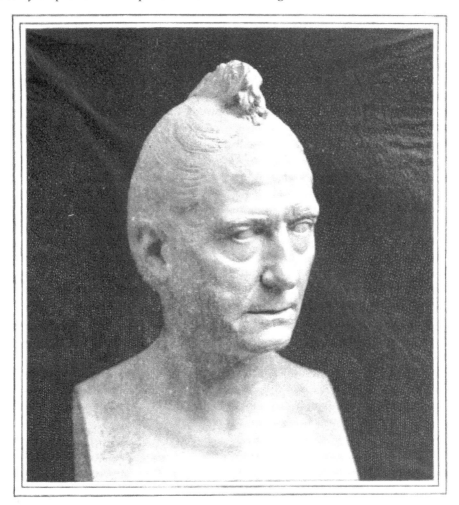

JOHN PAULDING

Age 59

The fact is, such a halo of romance and supposed chivalry has garlanded itself over André, owing to his youth and charming personality, that the best judgments are warped and influenced, in his favor, when they take up a consideration of his unhappy fate. Yet his case was an aggravated one. He entered upon the errand of a spy with his eyes wide open to its dangers and its consequences. He was taken red-handed, and suffered the penalty of his daring, after a trial, not by his peers, but by his superiors. His suppliant plea that he was unwittingly betrayed within our lines by the very man with whom he knew he was holding unlawful communication, and that he should be protected by the word and passes of the traitor Arnold, are pathetic in their puerility; yet his cause has not failed of advocates upon this plea. After all, it is merely the settling of a sentimental point in history, and the consensus of opinion is that André suffered justly and that posterity should "repeat with reverence the names of Van Wart, Paulding, and Williams."

The truth is, there is too much unnecessary iconoclasm abroad in regard to historic characters. Where false reputations have been built upon foundations laid by others, or impinge upon the honor due to another, it is meet and right that they should be exposed and honor be given to whom honor is due. But there is no such condition here; it is a mere attempt to tarnish one of the most important acts of the American Revolution in its far-reaching consequences, so that it shall be deprived of some of its brilliancy. On the present question we can do no better than accept the judgment of Washington—a man never carried away by his feelings, but always calm, judicial, and just. He wrote to Congress: "I do not know the party that took Major André, but it is said that it consisted only of a few militia, who acted in such a manner upon the occasion as does them the highest honor and *proves them to be men of great virtue*. As soon as I know their names I shall take pleasure in transmitting them to Congress." And later, in forwarding the proceedings of the Board of War, to Congress, he writes: "I have now the pleasure to communicate the names of the three persons who captured Major André and *who refused to release him notwithstanding the most earnest importunities and assurances of a liberal reward on his part*. Their names are John Paulding, David Williams, and Isaac Van Wart."

The master spirit of the three captors seems to have been John Paulding, who was the first of them to die, as also the first to have his mask taken by Browere. Indeed, his bust is from the earliest mask we have that Browere made, and is inscribed by the sculptor: "Made 1821 from the mould made in 1817." The latter was the year of the Tallmadge episode, and Paulding, when in New York in connection with that affair, was taken, by Alderman Percy Van Wyck, to Browere's house at No. 315 Broadway, where the life mask was made.

The attempt has also been made to throw discredit upon the service of the captors of André by underestimating their social position in the community in which they lived. This absurd but too common practice in a democracy like ours, where all men are supposed to be equal, can cut no figure here; for whatever may have been the station in life of Williams and Van Wart, who were kinsmen (the latter's mother and the former's father having been brother and sister), Paulding belonged to a family of consideration in his native State.

John Paulding was born in New York city in 1758, and died in Staatsburg, Dutchess county, New York, February 18, 1818. His brother, William Paulding, represented Suffolk county in the first provincial congress that met in New York city, May 23, 1775; was a member of the New York Committee of Safety, and commissary-general of the State troops. He, himself, served throughout the war of the Revolution, and was three times taken prisoner by the British, having escaped from his second capture only a few days before the adventure with André. His unswerving patriotism is therefore established by his personal service. Paulding was the one who actually made the arrest by seizing the bridle of André's horse, and he was the leader and spokesman on the occasion. Nearly a decade after his death, the corporation of the city of New York caused a monument to be erected over his grave, at Peekskill, when his nephew, William Paulding, then Mayor of New York, made the dedicatory address. Rear-Admiral Hiram Paulding—who, at the time of his death, October 20, 1878, was senior officer in the United States navy—was his son, and Commander Leonard Paulding, who commanded the *St. Louis*, the first ironclad vessel in the United States navy, in the war of the rebellion, was his grandson; while James Kirke Paulding, the collaborateur of Washington Irving, in the Salmagundi papers, and Secretary of the Navy under President Van Buren, was his nephew. Surely this brief family history is sufficient to set at rest any ridiculous squabbling as to his respectability and position in the community. He very possibly wore the stigma of poverty, in which case his refusal to release André, "notwithstanding the most earnest importunities *and assurances of a liberal reward*," only emphasizes him to have been, in the words of Washington, a man of "great virtue."

ISAAC VAN WART

Age 66

Isaac Van Wart, who next followed Paulding to the grave, died at Mount Pleasant, New York, on May 23, 1828, having been born, in Greenburg, sixty-eight years before. He was the youngest of the three captors. Van Wart was a West Chester farmer, and a staunch adherent to the cause of his country; and there is no more reason to throw doubt upon the purity of his motives in the great affair of his life than upon the motives of Paulding, which are beyond questioning. His social position also seems to be established by the fact, that he was a brother of Abraham Van Wart, Adjutant in the Continental line, whose son Henry married the youngest sister of Washington Irving. Van Wart's mask was made by Browere at Tarrytown in 1826, and until its discovery by the writer there was no likeness of him known to be in existence.

DAVID WILLIAMS

Age 75

David Williams, the eldest and the last survivor of the three, was born in Tarrytown, October 21, 1754, dying near Livingstonville, August 2, 1831. He served under Montgomery in the expedition to Canada, and remained actively in the service until disabled by frozen feet. Many of the details of the capture of André that we have, are from Williams's sworn statement, made on the day following, when everything was perfectly fresh in his mind. He passed the closing years of his life on a farm in the Catskills, that had belonged to the leader of Shays's rebellion, and it is still in the occupancy of Williams's descendants. A monument has been erected to his memory, by the State of New York, near Schoharie Court House.

Browere had great trouble in securing Williams's mask. Twice he went by sloop and on foot for this purpose to the latter's home at Schoharie, only to find the veteran absent. Finally, in 1829, Williams visited General Delavan, at Peekskill, and sent Browere word, whereupon the artist went thither and took the mask, the only portrait extant of the sturdy patriot.

Therefore to Browere's art,—or "process," whichever one pleases,—we owe, among other causes for congratulation, the possession of the only authenticated likenesses of Paulding, Williams and Van Wart, the three pure and unyielding patriots who captured the unfortunate André, and who, "leaning only on their virtue and an honest sense of their duty, could not be tempted by gold." Thereby they saved Washington and his army from capture, and possibly preserved the infant nation from a return to servitude. Each one of them received the thanks of Congress, and from the State of New York a two-hundred-acre farm. "Vincit amor patriæ."

V

DISCOVERY OF THE LIFE MASK OF JEFFERSON

HAD been familiar, for years, with the tragic story told by Henry S. Randall, in his ponderous life of President Jefferson,[2] of how the venerated sage of Monticello, within a year of his decease, was nearly suffocated, by "an artist from New York," by name Browere, who had attempted to take a mask of his living features; and how, in fear of bodily harm from the ex-President's irate black body-servant, "the artist shattered his cast in an instant," and was glad to depart quickly with the fragments which he was permitted to pick up.

This unvarnished tale, copied word for word, was put into the mouth of Clark Mills, the sculptor, by Ben Perley Poore, and published by him, some years later, under the caption of "Jefferson's Danger." With these statements fixed in my mind, I came across, while searching for information anent my article on the "Life Portraits of Thomas Jefferson,"[3] a letter from James Madison to Henry D. Gilpin, written October 25, 1827, in which Madison writes, respecting Jefferson's appearance, "Browere's bust in plaster, from his mode of taking it, will probably show a perfect likeness."[4]

I was struck by the utter inconsistency of Randall's circumstantial account of the shattered cast, picked up in fragments, with Madison's pointed observations upon "Browere's bust," as being in existence fifteen months after Jefferson's death.

The latter directly negatived the former.

This made it both interesting and important to ascertain the exact status of the subject, by tracing it to and from the fountain source, a task I found comparatively easy through the calendars of Jefferson and Madison Papers, in the State Department, at Washington. From an examination of these manuscripts, together with the newspapers of the time, it was clearly to be seen that Mr. Randall's method of writing history, was to accept and repeat irresponsible country gossip, rather than to turn to documents at his hand, that would explain and refute the gossip.

---

[2] Randall's "Life of Jefferson," 1858, Vol. III, p. 540.
[3] "McClure's Magazine," May, 1898.
[4] "Madison Papers," Vol. III, p. 594.

The existence at one time of the bust of Jefferson, from Browere's life mask, being thus established, the next and more difficult quest was to discover its whereabouts, if still extant. I instituted a systematic search, that gained for me among my friends the sobriquet of Sherlock Holmes, and my persistency was finally rewarded not only by the discovery of this bust of Jefferson, but also of all the other busts that had remained in Browere's possession at the time of his death. They were in the custody of a granddaughter of the artist, on a farm near Rome, New York.

The positive statement of Randall, frequently repeated by others, the last time unequivocally by Mr. Laurence Hutton, in his "Portraits in Plaster," that Browere's mask from Jefferson's face was *destroyed*, and the indisputable fact that the bust from the perfect mask *exists* and is here reproduced, cause the incidents connected with the taking of this original life mask, to have an importance that justifies recording them at length, so that there may remain no possibility for further question or doubt on the subject. My authorities are Jefferson, Madison and Browere, as preserved in their own autographs, in the State Department, at Washington.

Thomas Jefferson was born in 1743 and died in 1826, on the semi-centennial of the adoption of the immortal instrument of which he is the recognized father. Through the intercession of President Madison, his friend, neighbor and successor in the chair of state, Jefferson consented, in Browere's words, "to submit to the ordeal of my new and perfect mode of taking the human features and form." For this purpose Browere visited Monticello, on the fifteenth of October, 1825. At this time Jefferson was eighty-two years of age and was suffering the infirmities incident to his advanced years. During the operation, he was attended by his faithful man-servant Burwell, who prepared him for "the ordeal," by removing all of his clothing to the waist, excepting his undershirt, from which the sleeves were cut. He was then placed on his back, and the material applied down to the waist, including both arms folded across the body. The entire procedure lasted ninety minutes, with rests every ten or fifteen minutes, during which rests Jefferson got up and walked about. The material was on Jefferson's face for eighteen minutes, and the whole of the mould of his features was removed therefrom in three minutes. This was accomplished before the alarmed entrance of his granddaughters, the Misses Randolph, into the room. They were brought there by their brother, who had been peeping in at the window, and begging for admission, which was denied him. It was the exaggerated report of what young Randolph thought he saw, that induced the sudden entrance of his sisters, and this report found its way subsequently into the local newspapers of Virginia, with the remarkable result indicated.

The intrusion of the Randolphs into the room caused delay in removing other parts of the mould, and this did cause the venerable subject to feel a little faint and to experience some other discomforts. But Browere remained at Monticello overnight, dining with Jefferson and the Randolphs, and chatting with his host through the evening until bed-time, which would scarcely have been the case had the artist nearly suffocated and otherwise maltreated his subject, so that for his safety, the cast had to be shattered to pieces. But we do not have to speculate and surmise. We have direct and unimpeachable proof to the contrary.

The very day on which, according to Randall and his followers, the "suffocation" and "shattering" took place, Jefferson wrote:

> At the request of the Honorable James Madison and Mr. Browere of the city of New York, I hereby certify that Mr. Browere has this day made a mould in plaster composition from my person for the purpose of making a portrait bust and statue for his contemplated National Gallery. Given under my hand at Monticello, in Virginia, this 15th day of October, 1825.
>
> TH: JEFFERSON.

THOMAS JEFFERSON

Age 82

Four days later President Madison, who, with his wife, was Browere's next subject, writes: "A bust of Mr. Jefferson, taken by Mr. Browere from the person of Mr. Jefferson, has been submitted to our inspection and appears to be a faithful likeness." That Jefferson did suffer some inconvenience, from the application of the wet material, is undeniable. Three days after the taking of the mould he wrote to Madison: "I was taken in by Mr. Browere. He said his operation would be of about twenty minutes and less unpleasant than Houdon's method. I submitted without enquiry. But it was a bold experiment, on his part, on the health of an octogenary worn down by sickness as well as age. Successive coats of thin grout plastered on the naked head and kept there an hour, would have been a severe trial of a young and hale man."

But the newspapers had gotten hold of the "suffocation" and "shattering" story, and any one familiar with the newspapers of that day knows what a scarcity of news there was. Therefore the press over the land laid the Virginia papers tribute for this bit of sensationalism. Richmond, Boston and New York vied with each other in keeping the ball moving. But "those teachers of disjointed thinking," as Dr. Rush called the public press, were getting too rabid for Browere, so he published, in the Boston "Daily Advertiser" of November 30, 1825, a two-column letter, in which he calls the attack by the "Richmond Enquirer," the most virulent of his assailants, "a libel false in almost all its parts and which I am now determined to prove so by laying before the public every circumstance relating to that operation on our revered ex-president, Thomas Jefferson."

A copy of this published letter Browere sent to Jefferson under cover of the following important but effusive epistle:

New York, May 20, 1826.

Most Esteemed and venerable Sir:

As the poet says "there are strings in the human heart which once touched will sometimes utter dreadful discord." Per the public vehicles of information, the ex-President has perceived the very illiberal manner in which my character and feelings have been treated, and that of those of his honor have been unintentionally wounded. Mine have been publickly assaulted, upbraided and lacerated. And why? Because through the error of youth, I unwittingly, in a confidential letter to M. M. Noah, Esq., editor of the New York National Advocate, had written in a style either too familiar or that the whole of said letter (instead of extracts therefrom) had been made public. In my address to the Boston public, the ex-president will perceive I set down naught but facts. That I intended not to wound your feelings or those of the ladies at Monticello, I acknowledged the urbanity of Mr. Jefferson and the hospitality of his family. Possibly the ex-president is not aware that a young gentleman, one of his family, did, previous to my departure from Monticello, (the very afternoon of the day on which I took the bust) go to Charlottesville, and publickly declare I had almost killed Mr. Jefferson, first almost separating the ears, cutting the skull and suffocating him. What were my feelings? What! would not any man of spirit and enterprise resent such assertions and rebut them? I was in this state of feeling when I indited the letter to M. M. Noah, which letter I fear has forfeited me your confidence and regard. But a letter confidential and therefore not to be attributed as malign or censorious.

Your character I have always esteemed, and I now intend evidencing that regard by making a full-length statue of the "Author of the Declaration of American Independence," which (if the president be not in New York on the 4th of July next) I intend presenting for that day to the Honorable the Corporation of New York, to be publickly exhibited to all who desire to view the beloved features of the friend of science and of liberty.

The attitude of your statue will be standing erect; the left hand resting on the hip; the right hand extended and holding the unfolded scroll, whereon is written the Declaration of American Independence. If possible, History, Painting, Sculpture, Poetry and Fame will be attendant. The portrait busts of Washington, John Adams, Franklin, Madison, John Q. Adams, Lafayette, Clinton and Jay, will be on shields, hung on the column of Independence, surmounted with the figure of Victory. May you enjoy health, peace and competence. May the God of nature continue to shower down his choicest blessings on your head and finally receive you to himself is the prayer of your sincere friend,

J. H. I. BROWERE.

This communication Jefferson acknowledged, within a month of his decease, in a letter of such ruling importance in this connection, as it *settles the question forever*, that I am glad of the opportunity to publish it in full.

MONTICELLO, June 6, '26.

Sir:

The subject of your letter of May 20, has attracted more notice certainly than it merited. That the operé to which it refers was painful to a certain degree I admit. But it was short lived and there would have ended as to myself. My age and the state of my health at that time gave an alarm to my family which I neither felt nor expressed. What may have been said in newspapers I know not, reading only a single one and that giving little room to things of that kind. I thought no more of it until your letter brot. it again to mind, but can assure you it has left not a trace of dissatisfaction as to yourself and that with me it is placed among the things which have never happened. Accept this assurance with my friendly salutes.

TH: JEFFERSON.

Notwithstanding this "very kind and consolatory letter," as Browere had good reason to call it, the report that the venerable Jefferson had been nearly suffocated and otherwise maltreated by the artist, was so widely circulated that Browere's career was seriously affected by it; and so much easier is it to disseminate error than truth, that his hopes were not fulfilled that the publication of Jefferson's letter would, as he wrote to Madison, "in some manner turn the current of popular prejudice, which at present is great against my *modus operandi*."

In acknowledging Jefferson's letter of the 6th, Browere writes concerning the statue: "On the very day of the receipt of yours, the 13th inst., I had completed your full length statue (nudity) and to-morrow I intend, if spared, to commence dressing it in the costume you wore at the time of your delivery of the Declaration of American Independence. Understanding that your dress corresponded with that of Mr. Laurens, President of Congress in 1778, I have commenced the suit. But if Mr. Jefferson would condescend to give a full and explicit account of the form and colour of his dress, at that very interesting period, he will be conferring a particular favor on me and on the whole American Nation. Dispatch in forwarding the same will be pleasing to the Honorable the Common Council of New York, for whom I am preparing your statue for the 4th of July, 1826."

An examination of such of the New York newspapers of the period as could be found, fails to reveal any mention of this remarkable, colored and habited, statue of Jefferson, our whole knowledge of which is derived from the letters of the artist. It would seem to have belonged to the Eden Musée variety of freaks, from Browere's own description of it. Here is what he writes to Madison from New York, July 17, 1826: "You are aware that two months ago I tendered to the Common Council of New York, my services and those of my son to complete a full length figure or statue of Jefferson. The memorial was unanimously accepted and referred to the Committee on Arts and Sciences, who would superintend its being placed in the Banqueting Room of the Common Council, on the approaching anniversary or jubilee. Without money and without power I was enabled in five weeks of unremitting exertions, to finish and place it in the Hall, exactly at the hour of the dissolution of Mr. Jefferson." It may not be unamusing to read a description of his statue in the City Hall banqueting-room.

"His lofty and majestic figure standing erect; his mild blue and expressive eyes beaming with intelligence and good will to his fellow men. The scroll of the Declaration, which gave freedom to millions, clutched in his extended right hand, strongly contrasted with the decrepitude of his elder associate, the venerable John Adams, gave an effect to the whole which will not ever be forgotten here. His left hand resting on the hip, gave a carelessness yet dignified ease that pleased thousands. On his right hand was the portrait bust of the venerable Charles Carroll of Carrollton, like that of Adams, clothed with white drapery. Beside and behind these figures were placed various flowers and shrubbery. Immediately over the head of the author of the Declaration of American Independence hovered the American Eagle; a civic crown suspending from his beak was ready to drop on the temples and crown with immortal honors the wisest and best of men. His likeness is perfect. If the congratulations of Governor De Witt Clinton, His Honor the Mayor, the City authorities of New York and the general mass of reputable lives, can affix the seal of truth in likeness, rest assured the beloved features will not soon be forgotten.

"Now should the University of Virginia desire to erect in marble or bronze a statue to the memory of its founder be pleased, Sir, to note that I will be ready at all times to complete such a work. Moreover that, should appropriate funds at this period be lacking, it matters not: I will furnish one and await the pleasure of the institution for pecuniary emolument. All that would be required at first, would be a sufficiency to defray actual expenditures for materials and the indispensable requisites to the support of my young family. Should this proposition meet the approval of the visitors of the Virginia University and the citizens at large, a satisfactory answer will meet with my cordial thanks."

Evidently the University of Virginia did not accept Browere's proposition, as the only statue of its founder and architect, now to be seen there is an extremely bad one by a sculptor named Galt; and no trace of Browere's curious work has up to the present time been found. Save for the truth of history, silence concerning it would seem to have been most expedient for Browere's reputation as a serious artist.

Surely this story is as interesting as a romance, and but for fiction it might never have been told. How dare any man assume to write history and set down on his pages such statements, as did Randall about Browere's mask of the living Jefferson, without first exhausting every channel of inquiry and every means of search and research to ascertain the truth? The material that I have drawn from was as accessible to Mr. Randall as it has been to me; in fact, he claims to have used the Jefferson papers in his compilation. It is true we have acquired more exact and scientific methods of writing history than were in vogue when Randall wrote, a generation or more ago. Yet this will not excuse his positive misstatements and false assumptions. The existence of an opportunity for such severe criticism only serves to emphasize the great necessity of observing the inflexible rule: take nothing for granted and nothing at second hand, without the most careful investigation and scrutiny. If the standard of life's ordinary action should be the precept "Whatever is worth doing is worth doing well," with what intensified force does it apply to the writing of history! Pains, infinite pains, are the requisites for good work. Nothing meritorious is ever accomplished without hard labor. Toil conquers everything; without it, the result is at best uncertain. While it is some gratification to have set wrong right and done tardy justice to Browere's reputation, it is a far greater satisfaction to have rescued from oblivion and presented to the world his magnificent facsimile of the face and form of Thomas Jefferson.

VI

THREE GENERATIONS OF ADAMSES

HE allied families of Adams and Quincy are the only instances in this country, that present themselves to my mind, of hereditary ability manifesting itself and being recognized in the public service, for three and more generations. The Quincy family has done its work in local and more narrow spheres than the Adamses; yet Josiah Quincy, Jr., of Boston Port Bill fame, and his son, bearing the same name, who for so many years was at the head of Harvard University, have had a wide field for the spread of their influence. But the Adams family is the only one that has given father and son to the Presidential chair, and father, son, and grandson to the English mission. The series of double coincidences in the Adams family connected with missions to England and treaties with that power, is most curious. John Adams, just after having served as a commissioner to arrange the treaty of peace that concluded the Revolutionary War, was made minister to the court of St. James; his son John Quincy Adams, immediately after signing the treaty of Ghent, that concluded the war of 1812-15, was appointed minister to the same court; and his grandson, Charles Francis Adams, minister to England during the entire Civil War, took part in the treaty that disposed of the Alabama question.

John Adams was born in 1735 and died in 1826. The coincidences in his career, parallel with events in the career of Jefferson, are very remarkable. They were both on the committee of five to draft the Declaration of Independence; they both signed that American *Magna Charta*; they both represented this country in France; they both became successively Vice-President and then President of these United States, being the only signers of the Declaration of Independence thus elevated to the chair of state; and they both died, within a few hours of each other, on the fiftieth anniversary of the adoption of the Declaration of Independence. Is it possible that more curious historical parallels can be found in the lives of any two men?

From Monticello, the home of Jefferson, Browere journeyed to Quincy, the home of Adams, in order to secure a mask of the face of the distinguished nonagenarian. But the Virginian story of the maltreatment of Jefferson had gotten there before him, and it was with difficulty that Browere could persuade Mr. Adams to submit. However, the old Spartan finally yielded, and submitted not only once but twice, as appears by his certificate:

QUINCY, MASS., Nov. 23, 1825.

This certifies that John H. I. Browere of the city of New York, has yesterday and to-day made two Portrait bust moulds on my person and made a cast of the first which has been approved of by friends.

JOHN ADAMS.

JOHN ADAMS

Age 90

To this certificate, his son, Judge Thomas B. Adams, added a postscript:

"I am authorized by the ex-President to say that the moulds were made on his person without injury, pain or inconvenience."

The bust from the mask of old John Adams is, next to that of Jefferson, the most interesting of Browere's works. I do not mean for the subject, but for its truthful realism. There is an unhesitating feeling of real presence conveyed by Browere's busts that is given by no other likeness. They present living qualities and characteristics wanting in the painted and sculptured portraits of the same persons. Such a comparison is easily made in the instance of John Adams, for the same year as that in which Browere made his life masks, Gilbert Stuart painted his famous portrait of "John Adams at the age of ninety"; and Browere's bust will bear comparison with Stuart's portrait. I must tell a story connected with the painting of this portrait by Stuart, which, while a little out of place, especially as we have a chapter devoted to Gilbert Stuart, comes in better here than there. Stuart had painted a portrait of John Adams as a younger man. It is the familiar portrait of the great statesman by that artist. John Quincy Adams was desirous that Stuart should paint another of his father at the advanced age of ninety, and applied to the artist for the purpose. But Stuart was too old to go down to Quincy, and John Adams was too old to come up to Boston. Finally, Stuart agreed that he would go down to Quincy, for the purpose, if he were paid half of the price of the picture before he went. To this John Quincy Adams gladly assented, and Stuart went to Quincy and had the first sitting. Then John Quincy Adams could not get Stuart to go down for a second sitting, and, as his father was past ninety, he feared he might die before the picture was finished. He at last succeeded in getting Stuart to go down for a second sitting by paying him the balance of the price of the picture. Then the artist would not go down to finish it, and the only way John Quincy Adams got him to complete the portrait was by promising him, if he would make the journey and do the work, he would pay him the agreed price over again. This is only one of many illustrations of the character of the greatest portrait-painter this country has produced, and the peer of any portrait-painter who has ever lived.

Browere broke his journey from Virginia to Massachusetts by a rest at the country's capital, and while there he took a mask of the ruling President, John Quincy Adams, and one of his young son, Charles Francis Adams. It was this young man who wrote to Browere as follows:

WASHINGTON CITY, October (28), 1825.

> The president requests me to state to Mr. Browere that he will be able to give him two hours tomorrow morning at seven o'clock at his (Mr. Browere's) rooms on Pennsylvania Avenue. He is so much engaged at present that this is the only time he can conveniently spare for the purpose of your executing his portrait bust from life.

C. F. ADAMS.

John Quincy Adams, the sixth President of the United States, was born in Braintree, Massachusetts, July 11, 1767, and died in the Speaker's room of the House of Representatives at Washington, February 28, 1848. He has been called the most cultivated occupant that the Presidential chair has ever had; but his administration was unimportant, and he personally was the most unpopular man who has yet achieved the high office. He seems to have anticipated Whistler in the "gentle art of making enemies."

JOHN QUINCY ADAMS

Age 58

Not the least interesting of Browere's busts is the youthful head of Charles Francis Adams, made when Mr. Adams had just passed his eighteenth birthday, he having been born August 18, 1807, in Boston, where he died November 21, 1886. The services of Mr. Adams to his country, as minister to England from 1861 to 1868, covering the entire period of the war between the States, can never be forgotten or overestimated, and will remain among the foremost triumphs of American diplomacy.

It is certainly of curious interest to have busts of three generations, in one family, made by the same hand and within a few days of each other, as is the case with

Browere's casts of John, John Quincy, and Charles Francis Adams.

CHARLES FRANCIS ADAMS

Age 18

VII

MR. AND MRS. MADISON

"JIMMY" MADISON and his wife "Dolly" were prominent characters in social as well as in public life. He early made a name for himself by his knowledge of constitutional law, and acquired fame by the practical use he made of his knowledge, in the creation of the Constitution of the United States, and in its interpretation in the celebrated letters of the "Federalist." With the close of Washington's administration Madison determined to retire to private life, but shortly before this he met the coy North Carolina Quakeress, Dorothea Payn. She was at the time the young widow of John Todd, to whom she had been married not quite a year, and Madison made her his wife.

James Madison was born in 1751 and Dorothea Payn in 1772, but the score and one years' difference in their ages did not prevent them from enjoying a married life of two score and two years of unclouded happiness. Madison died in 1836, and was survived by Mrs. Madison for thirteen years.

Madison's temperament, like that of his young bride, was tuned to too high a pitch to be contented with quietness after the excitement incident to his earlier career. Therefore his retirement, like stage farewells, was only temporary, and he became afterward the fourth President of the United States. As we have seen, it was Madison who brought Browere to the notice of Jefferson, and Browere was commended to Madison in the following letter from General Jacob Brown, the land hero of the war of 1812, and later Commander-in-chief of the Army of the United States:

WASHINGTON CITY, Oct. 1st, 1825.

My Dear Sir:

Mr. Browere waits on you and Mrs. Madison with the expectation of being permitted to take your portrait busts from the life. As I have a sincere regard for him as a gentleman and a scholar, and great confidence in his skill as an artist (he having made two busts of myself), in the art which he is cultivating, I name him to you with much pleasure as being worthy of your encouragement and patronage. I am interested in having Mr. Browere take your likeness, for I have long been desirous to obtain a perfect one of you. From what I have seen and heard of Mr. Browere's efforts to copy nature, I hope to receive from his hands that desideratum in a faithful facsimile of my esteemed friend ex-President Madison. Be pleased to present my most respectful regards to Mrs. Madison, and believe me always

Your most devoted friend,
JACOB BROWN.

JAMES MADISON

Age 74

From this introduction Browere seems to have gained the friendship of Mr. and Mrs. Madison, who took more than an ordinary interest in the artist and his family. They were on terms of familiar intercourse, and an infant, born to Mrs. Browere, July 3, 1826, was, by Mrs. Madison's permission, named for her. Some years later this child accompanied her parents on an extended visit to Montpelier.

That Madison was satisfied with the result of Browere's skill is shown by the following:

> Per request of Mr. Browere, busts of myself and of my wife, regarded as exact likenesses, have been executed by him in plaister, being casts made from the moulds formed on our persons, of which this certificate is given under my hand at Montpelier, 19, October, 1825.
>
> JAMES MADISON.

"DOLLY" MADISON

Age 53

Mr. and Mrs. Madison each submitted to Browere's process a second time, which is sufficient evidence that the ordeal was not severe and hazardous. The bust of Madison is very fine in character and expression, but that of Mrs. Madison is of particular interest, as being the only woman's face handed down to us by Browere. Her great beauty has been heralded by more than one voice and one pen, but not one of the many portraits that we have of her, from that painted by Gilbert Stuart, aged about thirty, to the one drawn by Mr. Eastman Johnson, shortly before her death, sustains the verbal verdict of her admirers; and now the life mask by Browere would seem to settle the question of her beauty in the negative.

"Dolly" Madison was in her fifty and third year when Browere made his mask of her face, and she lived on for a quarter century. She has always been surrounded by an atmosphere of personal interest, not so much for what she was as for what she was supposed to be. She doubtless possessed a charm of manner that made her a most attractive hostess at the White House during her reign of eight years, in which particular she shares the laurels with the winsome wife of Mr. Cleveland.

VIII

CHARLES CARROLL OF CARROLLTON

THE last of the signers of the Declaration of Independence, to be gathered to his fathers, was the distinguished Marylander, Charles Carroll of Carrollton, who so signed his name to distinguish himself from a younger kinsman of the same name, his object being merely purposes of convenience, and not the patriotic purpose of identifying himself to the British, as is commonly stated. Charles Carroll was not a member of the Continental Congress when the Declaration of Independence was adopted, but took his seat a fortnight afterward, in time to sign the instrument with the rest of the sitting delegates, when it was placed before them on August 2, 1776.

Mr. Carroll died November 14, 1832, in his ninety-sixth year, and his last public act was to lay the corner-stone of the Baltimore and Ohio Railroad on July 4, 1828. From the description of his personal appearance at this time, as given by Hon. John H. B. Latrobe, it would seem as if it had been written of Browere's bust, so true is Browere's work to the life. Mr. Latrobe says: "In my mind's eye I see Mr. Carroll now—a small, attenuated old man, with a prominent nose and receding chin, [and] small eyes that sparkled when he was interested in conversation. His head was small and his hair white, rather long and silky, while his face and forehead were seamed with wrinkles."

At the present time, when foreign matrimonial alliances of high degree, with American women, are of almost daily occurrence, it is interesting to note that among the first American women to marry into the nobility of England were three granddaughters of the "signer," Charles Carroll of Carrollton. They were the children of his daughter, Mrs. Caton, and became respectively the Marchioness of Wellesley, the Duchess of Leeds, and Lady Stafford.

Browere, when he presented himself to Mr. Carroll for the purpose of making his mask, was armed with the following letter from the eminent scientist, Doctor Samuel Latham Mitchill, which contains the super-added endorsements of Archibald Robertson, Richard Riker and M. M. Noah:

CHARLES CARROLL OF CARROLLTON

Age 88

New York, July 8, 1825.

My dear Sir:

I approve your design of executing a likeness in statuary of the Honorable Charles Carroll of Carrollton. When you shall present yourself to him within a few days, I authorize you to employ my testimony in favor of your skill, having submitted more than once to your plastic operation. I know that you can perform it successfully without pain and within a reasonable time. The likenesses you have made are remarkably exact, so much so that they may be truly called facsimile imitations of the life. Your gallery contains so many specimens of correct casts that not only common observers, but even critical judges bear witness to your industry, genius and talents. I foresee that your collection of busts already well advanced and rapidly enlarging, will, if your labors continue, become a depositary of peculiar and intrinsic value. Without instituting any invidious comparison between sister arts, the professional branch under which you address Mr. Carroll, possesses, in my humble opinion, all the superiority that sculpture exercises over music and painting.

Yours, with kind feelings and fervent wishes for success,

SAMUEL L. MITCHILL.

IX

THE NATION'S GUEST,
LA FAYETTE

ILBERT MOTIER DE LA FAYETTE, who had fought side by side with Washington at Brandywine and at Yorktown, made his third and last visit to the United States in 1824. Landing at Castle Garden, in New York, on August 15th of that year, he set sail thirteen months later, on September 7th, 1825, to return to France, in the frigate *Brandywine*. He came as the invited guest of the nation, and during his sojourn here travelled over the whole country, visiting each one of the twenty-four States and receiving one continuous ovation.

At the request of the Common Council of the city of New York, La Fayette permitted Browere to make a cast of his head, neck and shoulders on July 11, 1825. For this purpose La Fayette visited Browere's workshop, in the rear of No. 315 Broadway, New York, accompanied by Richard Riker, Elisha W. King and Henry I. Wyckoff, a committee of the Common Council. The composition had been applied and had set, and Browere was about taking it off, when the clock struck, and one of the committee remarked that the hour for the corporation dinner in honor of La Fayette, and which he was to attend, had arrived. "*Sacré bleu!*" said La Fayette, starting up, "Take it off! Take it off!" which caused a piece to fall out from under one of the eyes. This accident, which necessitated a second sitting, led to some interesting correspondence.

New York, Tuesday 12 o'clock,
July 12, 1825.

Dear General:

We have just been to see your bust by Mr. Browere and have pleasure in saying it is vastly superior to any other likeness of General La Fayette, which as yet has fallen under our inspection. Indeed it is a faithful resemblance in every part of your features and form, from the head to the breast, with the exception of a slight defect about the left eye, caused by a loss of the material of which the mould was made. This defect or deficiency Mr. Browere assures us, and we have confidence in his assertion, that he can correct in a few minutes and without giving you any pain, provided you will again condescend to his operations, for a limited time. We should much regret that this slight blemish should not be corrected, which if not done will cause to us and to the Nation a continued source of chagrin and disappointment.

> Most truly your Friends
> RICHARD RIKER
> ELISHA W. KING
> HENRY I. WYCKOFF.

This letter was followed two days later by the following to Browere:

> NEW YORK 14th July 1825.

Dear Sir:

Every exertion has been made to get General La Fayette to spend half an hour with you, so the eye of his portrait bust be completed, but in vain. He has not had more than four hours each night to sleep, but has consented that you may take his mask in Philadelphia. He left New York this morning at eight o'clock and will be in Philadelphia on Monday next, where he will remain three days. It you can be present there on Monday or Tuesday at furthest, you can complete the matter. He has pledged his word. This arrangement was all that could be effected by

> Your friend
> ELISHA W. KING.

P. S. Previous to going get a line from the Recorder or Committee.

Upon this letter Browere has endorsed:

NOTE.—The subscribing artist met the General on Monday, in the Hall of Independence, Philadelphia, and Tuesday morning [July 19, 1825] from seven to eight o'clock was busy in making another likeness from the face and head of the General. At 4 P.M. of that day he finished the bust under the eye of the General and his attendant, and had the satisfaction then of receiving from the General the assurance that it was the only good bust ever made of him.

> JOHN H. I. BROWERE.

The result of the second trial was a likeness so admirable and of such remarkable fidelity, that General Jacob Morton, Rembrandt Peale, De Witt Clinton, S. F. B. Morse, John A. Graham, Thomas Addis Emmet and others, came forward and enthusiastically bore witness to its being "a perfect facsimile" of the distinguished Frenchman. The written commendations of Peale and Morse are notably interesting as the views of two brother artists, each of whom had painted a portrait of La Fayette. Rembrandt Peale, widely known by his composite portrait of Washington, writes:

THE MARQUIS DE LA FAYETTE

Age 67

NEW YORK August 10th 1825.

The singular excellence shown by Mr. Browere in his new method of executing Portrait busts from the life deserves the applause and patronage of his countrymen. The bust of La Fayette, which he has just finished, is an admirable demonstration of his talent in this department of the Fine Arts. The accuracy with which he has moulded the entire head, neck and shoulders from the life and his skill in finishing, render this bust greatly superior to any we have seen. It is in truth a "faithful and a living likeness." Of this I may judge having twice painted the General's portrait from the life, once at Paris and recently at Washington.

REMBRANDT PEALE.

Samuel Finley Breese Morse was, at the period of which we write, an artist of some reputation as a portrait-painter, and he was under commission, from the corporation of New York, to paint a whole-length portrait of La Fayette for the City Hall, where it now hangs. Its chief interest is as a study of costume; for if Browere's bust is "a perfect facsimile" of La Fayette's form and features, true to life, Morse's portrait is a caricature. That Morse was destined to greater ends than painting mediocre portraits, was shown, a decade later, by his invention of the magnetic electric telegraph, a discovery of such importance that while millions of human beings know Morse the inventor, not a dozen perhaps ever heard of Morse the painter. He damns his own portrait of La Fayette by the following commendation of Browere's bust:

NEW YORK August 15, 1825.

Being requested by Mr. Browere to give my opinion of his bust or cast from the person of General La Fayette, I feel no hesitation in saying it appears to me to be a perfect facsimile of the General's face.

SAML. F. B. MORSE.

These are certainly strong words coming from a rival artist and a man of Mr. Morse's character.

John A. Graham, who published a volume to prove that Horne Tooke was the author of the Letters of Junius, was one of the leading lawyers of New York. His closing words of eulogy upon the bust of La Fayette should have been, but unfortunately were not, prophetic. He wrote: "I have no doubt that the name of Browere, in virtue of this bust, will live as long as the memory of La Fayette shall be beloved and respected in America." On the contrary, the name of Browere was wholly and entirely forgotten and unknown, until brought to light, and publicly proclaimed, by the present writer, in the fall of 1897. So much for the stability of man's reputation!

X

DE WITT CLINTON

HEN Samuel Woodworth, the author of the well-known lines to the "Old Oaken Bucket," who was a close friend of Browere, entered the artist's workshop and caught a glimpse of the bust of De Witt Clinton, he made a gesture, as of restraint, and pronounced these impromptu lines:

"Stay! the bust that graces yonder shelf claims our regard.
It is the front of Jove himself;
The Majesty of Virtue and of Power,
Before which guilt and meanness only cower.
Who can behold that bust and not exclaim,
Let everlasting honor claim our Clinton's name!"

De Witt Clinton, who was born in 1769 and died in 1828, was the first recognized practical politician of this country. Apart from his immense service in pushing to completion the Erie canal, he was essentially a politician for what politics would yield. Consequently, he was always looked upon with distrust, and even his high private station was powerless to overcome this feeling. He posed as a connoisseur of the fine arts, was at one time President of the American Academy of Arts, and seems to have had a lofty appreciation of Browere's work. He wrote: "I have seen and examined with attention several specimens of busts executed by Mr. Browere in plaster, and have no hesitation in saying that their accuracy is equally surprising and gratifying. I feel pleasure in recommending the fidelity of his likenesses, and the skill with which they are executed, particularly the portrait bust of General La Fayette."

Of Clinton's own bust the eminent Irish patriot and American advocate, Thomas Addis Emmet, wrote to Browere:

New York July 6th 1826.

Sir:

If my opinion as to the merits of the portrait busts I have seen of your workmanship, can be of any advantage to you, it is entirely at your service. I really think them all entitled to great praise for fidelity of expression and accuracy of resemblance. Those of General La Fayette and Governor Clinton are, as far as I can judge, the most perfect likenesses of the originals that have as yet been presented to the public.

I am, Dear Sir, your obt Servt
THOMAS ADDIS EMMET.

DE WITT CLINTON

Age 56

XI

HENRY CLAY

ENRY CLAY, who wore the appellation, conferred upon Pitt, of "the Great Commoner," long before it was given to Mr. Gladstone, has left behind him perhaps the most distinct personality of any of the statesmen of his era. Where Daniel Webster counted his admirers by hundreds, Henry Clay was idolized by thousands; the one appealing to the head and the other to the heart. His strongly marked features are familiar to every one, from the scores of portraits of him to be found here, there, and everywhere; while there are, living to-day, a large number of people who knew Clay in the flesh; so that Browere's bust of him needs no perfunctory certificate to assure of its truthfulness. It is certainly human to a wonderful degree, and there could scarcely be any truer portraiture than this, wherein we have the very features of the living man down to the minutest detail.

Clay was of striking physique. He was quite tall, nearly six feet two inches, rather sparsely built, with a crane-like neck that he endeavored to conceal by his collar and stock. He had an immense mouth, phenomenal for size as well as shape, and kindly blue eyes which were electrical when kindled. Yet he was so magnetic in his power over men that when he was defeated for the Presidency, thousands of his Whig followers wept as they heard the news.

Henry Clay was born in Hanover county, Virginia, April 12, 1777, and died at Washington, June 29, 1852, preceding his compeer Webster to the grave by only a few months. On reaching his majority, he removed to Lexington, Kentucky, which became his future home, although he was so rarely out of public life that he was comparatively little there. Having chosen the law for his profession, he was admitted to the bar, and before attaining his thirtieth year, was sent to the Senate of the United States. He was strenuous in his support of home industries, and endeavored by legislation to enforce upon legislators the wearing of homespun cloths. So ardent was he in this, that his course led to a duel with Humphrey Marshall, in which both were slightly wounded.

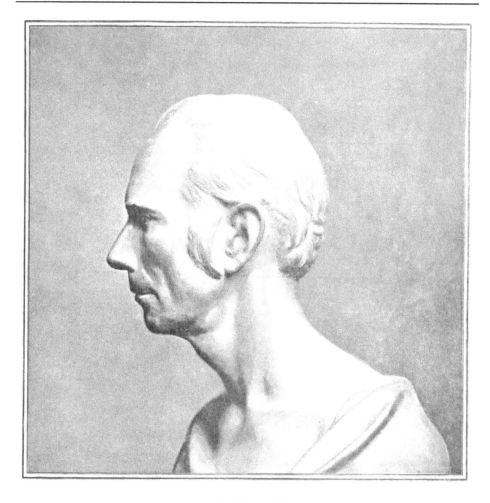

HENRY CLAY

Age 48

At the close of the war of 1812, Clay was one of the commissioners appointed to negotiate the treaty of peace with Great Britain, and as such signed the Treaty of Ghent. He was known as "the great Pacificator," from his course in the events that led to the Missouri Compromise and later averted Southern "nullification." He was an active and bitter opponent of Andrew Jackson, and supported John Quincy Adams against him for the Presidency, his reward being the portfolio of State; but there was no bargain and corruption about this business as his enemies claimed and which haunted Clay's political career throughout the rest of his life. He was an ambitious man, and his failure to reach the goal of his ambition—the presidential chair—was a fatal blow.

Clay was undoubtedly one of the greatest orators this country has produced, and a man with much natural ability, but little study and cultivation. His name is one to conjure with in old Kentucky, and it is with a moist eye that personal reminiscences of Clay are related out there in the blue grass State, even at this day, nearly half a century after his decease.

XII

AMERICA'S MASTER PAINTER,
GILBERT STUART

NE artist, and he easily the first of American painters, did not deny to Browere and his works the merit that was their due. On the contrary, he saw the fidelity and great value of these life masks, and gave practical encouragement to the maker of them by submitting to his process and by giving a certificate of approval. He did this, not so much that his living face might be transmitted to posterity, as to test the truth of the newspaper reports of the suffering and danger experienced by the venerable and venerated Jefferson, and thus by his example encourage others to go and do likewise. The result was the superb head of Gilbert Stuart, herewith reproduced from the original bust, in the Redwood Library, at Newport, Rhode Island. This noble action of Stuart must have been as light out of darkness to Browere.

Upon the completion of the mask, from which this bust was made, Stuart gave to Browere the following emphatic certificate:

BOSTON November 29th 1825.

Mr. Browere, of the city of New York, has this day made a portrait bust of me from life, with which I am perfectly satisfied and which I hope will remove any illiberal misrepresentations that may deprive the nation from possessing like records of more important men.

G. STUART.

The "illiberal misrepresentations" referred to were of course the reported inconveniences that Jefferson had suffered; and praise such as this, from Stuart, is, as approbation from Sir Hubert Stanley, praise indeed.

A few days afterward the Boston "Daily Advertiser" announced: "The portrait bust of Gilbert Stewart, Esq., lately executed by Mr. Browere, will be exhibited by him at the Hubard Gallery, this evening. This exhibition is made by him for the purpose of showing that he can present a perfect likeness, and he will prove at the same time, by the certificate of Mr. Stewart, that the operation is without pain."

Two days later the local press fairly teemed with laudatory notices of Browere's work. The Boston "American" said: "This bust has been adjudged by all who have examined it and are acquainted with the original to be a striking and perfect resemblance." The "Commercial Gazette" said: "It is a fine likeness, in truth we think the best we ever saw of any one. We particularly enquired of Mr. Stuart's family if he suffered by any difficulty of breathing or if the process was in any degree painful, and were assured that there was nothing of an unpleasant or painful nature in it."

Considering Stuart's eminence in art, a position fully recognized in his lifetime, and his irascible temper and unyielding character, such action as his toward Browere, not only in submitting to have the mask taken, but in certifying to it and permitting it to be publicly exhibited for the benefit of Browere's reputation, speaks volumes of the highest authority in support of the workman and his work.

GILBERT STUART

Age 70

Stuart's daughter, Jane, who died at Newport, in 1888, at a very advanced age, and was as "impossible" in some respects as was her distinguished father, remembered well the incident of the mask being taken, and testified to its marvellous life-speaking qualities. Having lost all knowledge of its whereabouts, she searched for years in the hope of finding it, since she looked upon it as the next thing to having her father before her. Finally, in the Centennial year, it was discovered in the possession of Browere's son, and was purchased by Mr. David King, of Newport, as a present for Miss Stuart. But Miss Stuart felt that her little cottage, so well remembered by many visitors to Newport, was no place for so big a work, and desired that it might be placed in a public gallery, which wish Mr. King complied with, by presenting it to the Redwood Library, at Newport, where it may be seen by all interested in Stuart or in Browere's life masks. Jane Stuart is the subject of Colonel Wentworth Higginson's charming paper, "One of Thackeray's Women," in his volume of Essays entitled "Concerning All of Us."

Gilbert Stuart was born in what was called the Narragansett country, on December 3, 1755. The actual place of his birth is now called Hammond Mills, near North Kingston, Rhode Island, about nine miles from Narragansett Pier; and the old-fashioned gambrel-roofed, low-portalled house, in which the future artist first saw light, still stands at the head of Petaquamscott Pond. The snuff-mill set up by Gilbert Stewart, the father of the painter, who had come over from Perth, in Scotland, at the suggestion of a fellow Scotchman, Doctor Thomas Moffatt, to introduce the manufacture of snuff into the colonies, was located, by the race, immediately under the room in which Stuart was born, both being part of the same building, so that Stuart's excuse for taking snuff, that he was born in a snuff-mill, is literally true.

When four months old, the third and youngest child of the snuff-grinder and his beautiful wife, Elizabeth Anthony, was carried, on Palm Sunday, to the Episcopal church and baptized "Gilbert Stewart." The significance of this record is found in the orthography of the surname and in the limitation of the baptismal name. Stuart's name will be found in print quite frequently as "Gilbert Charles Stuart," and I have seen it as "Charles Gilbert Stuart"; and the Jacobin leaning of his Scotch sire, is commonly supported by the naming of the child for the last of the Royal Stuarts, the romantic Prince Charlie. This pretty legend, built to support unreliable tradition, is blown to the winds by the prosaic church record, which shows that the artist's orthography was an assumption, and his name simply Gilbert Stewart. That this plebeian spelling of the royal name, was not an error or accident of the scribe who made it, is proved by signatures of the snuff-grinder which have come down to us.

Stuart's parents early removed to Newport, where the son had the advantage of tuition in English and Latin, from the assistant minister of venerable Trinity parish; but in his boyhood Stuart seems to have shown none of those dominant characteristics which later were so strongly developed both in the artist and in the man, unless it may be the predilection for pranks and practical jokes that early manifested itself.

The earliest picture that can be recognized as from the brush of Gilbert Stuart, is a pair of Spanish dogs belonging to the famous Dr. William Hunter, of Newport, which Stuart is said to have painted when in his fourteenth year; and what are claimed to be his first portraits, those of Mr. and Mrs. Bannister, have been so nearly destroyed by "restoration," that nothing of the original work remains to show any merit the pictures may have possessed.

Stuart's first instruction in art was received from Cosmo Alexander, a Scotchman, who passed a few years in the colonies painting a number of interesting portraits in the affected, perfunctory manner of the period. Of Alexander nothing was known until recent investigations by the writer discovered him to be a great-grandson of George Jamesone, whom Walpole calls "the Vandyke of Scotland." Alexander took Stuart, then in his eighteenth year, back with him to Scotland, to acquire a greater knowledge of art than was possible in the colonies at that time; and Stuart is claimed to have been at this period a student at the University of Glasgow. But this tradition, like that previously mentioned, is shattered, as tradition almost always is shattered, by the cold, unimaginative record, which fails to show his name on the matriculation register.

Alexander died not long after reaching Edinburgh, and Stuart was left, according to his biographers, in the care of Alexander's friend, "Sir George Chambers," who "quickly followed Alexander to the grave," leaving Stuart without protection. But this story is manifestly without foundation, as there *was* no "Sir George Chambers" at the period considered. There was, however, a Scotch painter of some repute, Sir George Chalmers, of Cults, who had married either a sister or a daughter of Cosmo Alexander; and this Sir George Chalmers is doubtless the person intended, although he lived on until 1791, so that it could not have been his demise that threw Stuart upon his own resources, which, being few, necessitated his working his way home, on a collier, after a few months' absence.

Stuart returned to America from Scotland at a period of intense excitement. The Boston Port bill had just been received, assuring what the Stamp Act had initiated, and the tories and the patriots were being marshalled according to their particular bias. It was not a time for the peaceful arts. It was the time for action and for town meetings. Before the echoes of Lexington and Concord had died away, "Gilbert Stewart the snuff-grinder" hied himself away to Nova Scotia, leaving his wife and family behind. At this epoch Gilbert Stuart, the future painter, was in his twentieth year, and apparently had inherited from his father sentiments of loyalty to the Crown, so that instead of going forth to battle for his native land, as many no older than he did, he embarked for England, the day before the action at Bunker Hill, with the ostensible object of seeking the Mecca of all of our early artists, the studio of Benjamin West.

Once in London, Stuart's object to seek instruction in painting from West, seems to have weakened, and he remained in the great metropolis nearly two years before he knocked at the Newman-street door of the kindly Pennsylvanian. These months were occupied chiefly with a sister art in which Stuart was most proficient. He loved music more than he loved painting—a taste that never forsook him. He played upon several instruments, but his favorites were the organ and the flute; indeed the story has come down that his last night in Newport, before sailing, was spent in playing the flute under the window of one of its fair denizens.

This knowledge of music stood Stuart in good stead when an unknown youth in an unknown land. A few days after his arrival in London, hungry and penniless, he passed the open door of a church, through which there came to his ear the strains of a feebly played organ. He ventured in and found the vestry sitting in judgment upon several applicants for the position of organist. Receiving permission to enter the competition, he was selected for the position at a salary of thirty pounds, after having satisfied the officials of his character, by reference to Mr. William Grant, whose whole-length portrait Stuart afterward painted.

Having some kind of subsistence assured him by the position of organist he thus secured, Stuart began that desultory dallying with art which later often left him without a dry crust for his daily bread. While his work was always serious, his temperament never was, and he seems to have played cruel jokes upon himself, as carelessly as he did upon others. For two years his career is almost lost to art; only once in a while did he gather himself together to work at his painting. He had, however, to a marked degree, that odd resource of genius which enabled him to work best and catch up with lost time when under the spur of necessity. In later days, with sitters besieging his door, he would turn them away, one by one, until the larder was empty and there was not a penny left in the purse; then he would go to work and in an incredibly short time produce one of his masterpieces.

Such was the character, in outline, of the man who went to London to study under West, and, after reaching the metropolis, let two years slip by him without seeking his chosen master. Finally he went to the famous American and was received as a pupil and as a member of the painter's family, in true apprentice style. Just what Stuart learned from West it is difficult to imagine;—unless it was how not to paint. For, without desiring or meaning to join in the hue and cry of to-day against the art of West, but on the contrary, protesting against the clamor which fails to consider the conditions that existed in his time and therefore fails to do him the justice that is his due, there is surely nothing in the work of the one to suggest anything in the work of the other.

For five long and doubtless weary years Stuart plodded under the guidance of his gentle master until, tired of doing some of the most important parts of West's royal commissions, for which his remuneration was probably only his keep and tuition, without even the chance of glory, he broke away and opened a studio for himself in New Burlington Street. If Stuart did gain little in art from West, he gained much of the invaluable benefit of familiar intercourse with persons of the first distinction, who were frequenters of the studio of the King's painter. This was of great advantage to the young artist when he set up his own easel, and many of these men became his early sitters.

Stuart, while domiciled with West, drew in the schools of the Royal Academy, attended the lectures of the distinguished William Cruikshank on anatomy, and listened to the discourses delivered by Sir Joshua Reynolds on painting. Later on he painted the portraits of each of these celebrated men, and did enough individual work to indicate the quality of the artistic stuff that was in him, awaiting an opportunity to manifest itself. In 1777, the year Stuart went to West, he made his first exhibition at the Royal Academy. His one contribution is entered in the catalogue of that year merely as "A Portrait." It is not improbable that this was a portrait of his fellow countryman and early friend, Benjamin Waterhouse, of Cambridge, Massachusetts, who preceded Stuart to London only a short time, and who seems to have remained the artist's chum during their sojourn in the English capital. A portrait of Doctor Waterhouse, by Stuart, was given by the Doctor's widow, to the Redwood library, at Newport, together with Stuart's self-portrait, wearing a large hat, and dated on the back, 1778. These two portraits are evidently of a contemporaneous period.

In 1779 Stuart exhibited, at the Royal Academy, three pictures: "A Young Gentleman," "A Little Girl," and "A Head." In 1781 he showed "A Portrait from Recollection since Death," and in 1782 made his last exhibition there, sending a "Portrait of an Artist," and "A Portrait of a Gentleman Skating." This last picture, although painted so early in his career, has been considered Stuart's *chef-d'œuvre*. It is a whole-length portrait of Mr. William Grant, of Congalton, skating in St. James Park. Mr. Grant was the early friend who bore testimony to Stuart's character, whereby Stuart gained the organist's position soon after his arrival in London; and the story has come down that Mr. Grant, desiring to help Stuart, determined to sit for his portrait, and went to Stuart's room for a sitting. The day was crisp and cold, and the conversation, not unnaturally, turned upon skating, a sport much enjoyed by both painter and sitter, each being rarely skilful at it. Finally paints and brushes were put away, and the two friends started forth to skate. Stuart was so struck with the beauty and rhythm of his companion's motion that he determined to essay a picture of him thus engaged. The original canvas was abandoned and a new one begun, showing Mr. Grant not merely upon skates, but actually skating; and the latent force of the graceful undulating motion has been rendered with a skill and ability that at once put Stuart in the front rank of the great portrait-painters of his day.

The remarkable merit of this picture and the wilful unreasonableness of painters in not signing their works, were curiously shown at the exhibition of "Pictures by the Old Masters," held at Burlington House, in January of 1878. In the printed catalogue of the collection this picture was attributed to Gainsborough, and attracted and received marked attention. A writer in the "Saturday Review," speaking of the exhibition, remarks: "Turning to the English school, we may observe a most striking portrait in number 128, in Gallery III. This is set down as 'Portrait of W. Grant, Esq., of Congalton, skating in St. James Park. Thomas Gainsborough, R. A. (?)' The query is certainly pertinent, for, while it is difficult to believe that we do not recognize Gainsborough's hand in the graceful and silvery look of the landscape in the background, it is not easy to reconcile the flesh tones of the portrait itself with any preconceived notion of Gainsborough's workmanship. The face has a peculiar firmness and decision in drawing, which reminds one rather of Raeburn than of Gainsborough, though we do not mean by this to suggest in any way that Gainsborough wanted decision in either painting or drawing when he chose to exercise it."

The discussion as to the authorship of this picture waxed warm, the champions of Raeburn, of Romney, and of Shee, contending with those of Gainsborough for the prize, which contention was only set at rest by a grandson of the subject coming out with a card that the picture was by "the great portrait-painter of America, Gilbert Stuart." And to Stuart it did justly belong.

With the success of this portrait of Mr. Grant, Stuart was launched upon the sea of prosperity, and to himself alone, and not to want of patronage or lack of opportunity, is due his failure to provide against old age or a rainy day. For a while he lived like a lord, in reckless extravagance. Money rolled in upon him, and he spent it lavishly, without a thought for the morrow. His rooms were thronged with sitters, and he received prices for his work second only to those of Reynolds and of Gainsborough. He was on the best footing with his brethren of the brush, and with Gainsborough, his senior by more than a quarter of a century, he painted a whole-length portrait of Henry, Earl of Carnarvon, in his robes, which has been engraved in mezzotinto by William Ward, with the names of the two painters inscribed upon the plate. This alone shows the estimation in which Stuart was held by his contemporaries, and it would be most interesting to know which parts were the work of Stuart and which were due to his famous collaborator.

About this period Boydell was in the midst of the publication of his great Shakespeare gallery, to which the first artists of the day contributed, and Stuart was commissioned by the Alderman, to paint, for the gallery, portraits of the leading painters and engravers who were engaged upon the work. Thus, for Boydell, he painted the superb half-length portraits of his master West, and of the engravers Woollett and Hall, now in the National Portrait Gallery, St. Martin's Place, London. He painted, also for Boydell, his own portrait, and portraits of Reynolds, Copley, Gainsborough, Ozias Humphrey, Earlom, Facius, Heath, William Sharp, Boydell himself, and several others. Stuart was an intimate friend of John Philip Kemble, and painted his portrait several times; one picture is in the National Portrait Gallery, and another, as *Richard III.*, which has been engraved by Keating, did belong to Sir Henry Halford.

Other prominent sitters to Stuart in London were Hugh, Duke of Northumberland, the Lord Percy of the Battle of Bunker Hill; Admiral Sir John Jervis, afterward Earl St. Vincent; Isaac Barré; Dr. Fothergill, and the Dukes of Manchester and of Leinster. From these names alone it can be seen that Stuart was in touch with persons of the highest consideration, and they were not only his patrons, but his friends. He kept open house, dispensing a princely hospitality. The story has been handed down that he led off with a dinner of forty-two, composed of the choice spirits of the metropolis. He was so charming as a host, and had gathered together such delightful guests, that it was suggested the same party should meet frequently, which proposition Stuart accepted, by arranging that six of them should dine with him each day of the week, without special invitation, the six first arriving to be the guests of the day, until the entire forty-two had again warmed their legs under his mahogany. Such prodigality as this, for a young artist, shows what Stuart's temperament was, and points as surely to the pauper's grave as though it was there yawning open before him.

Stuart was five feet ten inches in height, with fine physique, brown hair, a ruddy complexion, and strongly marked features. He dressed with elegance, which was possible at that period, and notwithstanding his biting sarcasm, keen wit, and searching eye, was a great favorite with the fair sex. In his thirty-first year he selected Miss Charlotte Coates, the daughter of a Berkshire physician, for his partner through life, and on May 10, 1786, they were married.

Stuart remained in London until 1788, when he was induced to visit Ireland and open a studio in Dublin. Here he kept up the same style of living he had indulged in before he left London and was in high favor with the Irish, painting some of his most elaborate portraits at this time; but, although fully employed and receiving the highest prices for his pictures, he was always without money. So poor was he, indeed, that when he returned to this country, in 1792, he had not the means to pay for his passage and engaged to paint the portrait of the owner of the ship as its equivalent. He landed in New York towards the close of the year; and although the tradition has been handed down that the cause of his returning to America, was his desire to paint the portrait of Washington, it seems, considering that he waited two years before visiting Philadelphia for the purpose, that the remark of Sir Thomas Lawrence may not have been without foundation. The latter, upon hearing this reason assigned, is related by Leslie to have said: "I knew Stuart well and I believe the real cause of his leaving England was his having become tired of the inside of our prisons." Whatever the real cause was that brought the artist home, we may congratulate ourselves that he came to live among us at the period that he did, for he was then in the fulness of his powers, and the pictures that he painted between this time and his removal to Boston, in 1805, are the finest productions of his brush on this side of the water.

Gilbert Stuart went to reside in Philadelphia about New Year, 1795. There he painted his famous life portraits of Washington, three in number, but I have written so often and so much on this subject that I shall content myself with this bare mention.[5] There also he painted the portraits of the famous men and of the beautiful women that have helped most to place his name so high up on the pillar of fame. That Stuart was a master in the art of portrait-painting it needs no argument to prove; his works are the only evidence needed, and they establish it beyond appeal. In his portraits the men and women of the past live again. Each individual is here, and it was Stuart's ability to portray the individual that was his greatest power. Each face looks at you and fain would speak, while the brilliant and animated coloring makes one forgetful of the past. The "Encyclopædia Britannica," a forum beyond dispute, says: "Stuart was pre-eminent as a colourist, and his place, judged by the highest canons in art, is unquestionably among the few recognized masters of portraiture."

Stuart had two distinct artistic periods. His English work shows plainly the influence of his English contemporaries, and might easily be mistaken, as it has been, for the best work of Romney or of Gainsborough. But his American work, almost the very first he did after his return to his native soil, proclaims aloud the

---

[5] *Vide* "Stuart's Lansdowne Portrait of Washington," in Harper's Magazine, Aug., 1896.

virility and robustness of his independence. The rich, juicy coloring so marked in his fine portraits painted here, replaces the tender pearly grays so predominant in his pictures painted there. The delicate precision of his early brush gives way to the masterful freedom of his later one. His English portraits might have been limned by Romney or by Gainsborough, but his American ones could have been painted only by Gilbert Stuart. This greatest of American painters died in Boston, July 27, 1828, and was interred in an unmarked grave in the Potter's Field.

XIII

DAVID PORTER,
UNITED STATES NAVY

HILE this country and the world are yet enthralled by the magical victories won by the American navy over the fleets of Spain, it is instructive to recall how the exploits of Uncle Sam's boys, on the seas, have always bordered on the marvellous. The doings of Paul Jones in the Revolutionary War, and of Truxtun in the war with France; of Decatur and of Preble in the war with Tripoli; of Bainbridge and of Stewart, and of Hull and of Perry, in the second war with England; and of Farragut and of Jouett and of Cushing in the war between the States, seem, each one, too incredible to have a like successor, yet nothing heretofore in naval warfare has approached the victories of Dewey and of Sampson. With all these glittering names, we have still another name the peer of the best, possessing in addition the spur of naval heredity—the name of Porter.

There have been three officers of high rank in the United States navy bearing the name of David Porter. The first served the Continental Congress; his son, born in 1780, gave the best years of his life to his country on the sea; and his grandson, after having four times received the thanks of Congress for his services during the Civil War, died at the head of the navy, with the rank of Admiral, in 1891. David Porter, second of the name, began his naval career in action, having been, at the age of eighteen, appointed a midshipman on board the frigate *Constellation*, and with her, soon after, participated in the fight where the French frigate *L'Insurgente* was captured by Truxtun with the loss of one man killed and two men wounded. Porter subsequently distinguished himself in the war with Tripoli, was promoted to a captaincy, and early in the war of 1812 sailed from New York, in command of the *Essex*, on one of the most eventful cruises ever had by a man-of-war. His first feat was to capture the *Alert*, in an engagement of eight minutes, without any loss or damage to his ship; and so well directed was the fire of the *Essex*, that the *Alert* had seven feet of water in her hold when she surrendered. This was the first British war vessel taken in the conflict. Porter then turned his attention to the destruction of the English whale-fishery in the Pacific Ocean, and sailed on this errand, around the Horn, for Valparaiso. He made such havoc with the British shipping that the loss footed up to two million and a half of dollars and four hundred men prisoners.

COMMODORE DAVID PORTER

Age 45

The British sent two vessels, with picked crews of five hundred men and a combined armament of eighty-one guns, to search for the *Essex* (mounting only thirty-two guns and with a crew of two hundred and fifty-five men), with instructions that neither ship should engage her singly. They found her in the neutral harbor of Valparaiso, where she was attacked, in defiance of all neutrality laws; and after one of the most desperate engagements in naval history, lasting two hours and a half, the *Essex* was forced to surrender. Upon his return home, Captain Porter was received with distinction and given the thanks of Congress and of several of the States. He retired from the navy, in 1826, to take command of the Mexican navy, from which he withdrew three years later, was subsequently appointed consul-general to the Barbary States, then *chargé d'affaires* at Constantinople, and later minister resident, which office he held at the time of his death.

It was but a short time before Porter's retirement from the navy that Browere took his life mask, and the toss of the head and the determined mouth show the qualities that made up David Porter's character. The spirited pose of this bust is quite remarkable in a life mask, and would seem to indicate that Browere's material must have been, at least in some degree, flexible. Porter was very enthusiastic over Browere's work, as may be seen from the following letter to Major Noah:

MERIDIAN HILL, 18th Sept. 1825.

Dear Sir:

By means of epistolary introduction I have had the pleasure of becoming acquainted with John H. I. Browere, Esq., a young and deserving artist of your city. Agreeably to your and my friends' requests, I consented to sit for my portrait bust, which has been executed by him according to his novel and perfect mode. Mr. Browere has succeeded to admiration. Nothing can be more accurate and expressive; in fact, it was impossible that it could be otherwise than a perfect facsimile of my person, owing to the peculiar neatness and dexterity which guide his scientific operation. The knowledge and dexterity of Mr. Browere in this branch of the Fine Arts is surprising, and were I to express my opinion on the subject, I should recommend every one who wished to possess a perfect likeness of himself or friends to resort to Mr. Browere in preference to any other man. His portrait busts are *chef d'œuvres* in the plastic art, unequalled for beauty and correct delineation of the human form. To those to whom a saving of time is important, Mr. Browere's method must receive the preference, were it solely on that ground. As to the effect of the operation, none need apprehend the least danger or inconvenience; it is perfectly safe and not disagreeable, for while the plastic material is applying to the skin, a sensation both harmless and agreeable produces a pleasant glow or heat somewhat similar to that which is felt on entering a warm bath; neither does the composition affect the eyes, which are covered with it. Too much commendation of Mr. Browere's rare and invaluable invention cannot be made. May he derive benefits from his art equal to his merit. Hoping to have the pleasure of seeing my friends in New York during the course of a few weeks, I remain, Dear Sir,

Your obt. servant
DAVID PORTER.

XIV

RICHARD RUSH

THE clean-cut features of Richard Rush recall a statesman and a scholar of "ye olden tyme." Born in Philadelphia, the eldest son of that signer of the Declaration of Independence who, both politician and physician, has been termed the Sydenham of America,— Doctor Benjamin Rush,—and a kinsman of William Rush, the first American sculptor, mentioned in the second chapter of this book,—Richard Rush was bred to the bar, and gained distinction, soon after attaining his majority, by his defence of William Duane, the editor of the "Aurora" newspaper, accused of libelling Governor McKean. When only thirty he entered public life by becoming Attorney-General of Pennsylvania, and at thirty-four was a member of the cabinet of President Madison, as Attorney-General of the United States. Three years later, he was for a brief period Secretary of State, and then minister from the United States to Great Britain, being recalled, in 1825, to become Secretary of the Treasury under John Quincy Adams. It was at this period that Browere made his mask. Rush was subsequently candidate for Vice-President on the ticket with John Quincy Adams when Mr. Adams sought a second term.

The career of Richard Rush was not only public, but it was important, and not the least of his wide-spread benefits were his successful efforts in securing for this government the munificent legacy of James Smithson; this was the foundation upon which has been reared the Smithsonian Institution, which has done so much for scientific pursuits in this country. James Smithson was a natural son of Hugh Smithson, Duke of Northumberland, and died in Genoa, June 27, 1829, aged about seventy-five years. He was a graduate of Oxford, and took up the study of natural philosophy, for his expertness in several branches of which he was made a member of the Royal Society and of the French Institute. He travelled extensively, and formed a very valuable cabinet of minerals which came into possession of the Institute founded by his liberality, but which was unfortunately destroyed in the Smithsonian fire of 1865.

Smithson's illegitimate birth seems to have engendered a desire for posthumous fame, as he wrote: "The best blood of England flows in my veins; on my father's side I am a Northumberland, on my mother's I am related to kings; but it avails me not. My name shall live in the memory of man when the titles of the Northumberlands and the Percys are extinct and forgotten." To carry out this desire he bequeathed his whole property, after the expiration of a life estate, "to the United States for the purpose of founding an institution at Washington, to be called the Smithsonian Institution, for the increase and diffusion of knowledge among men."

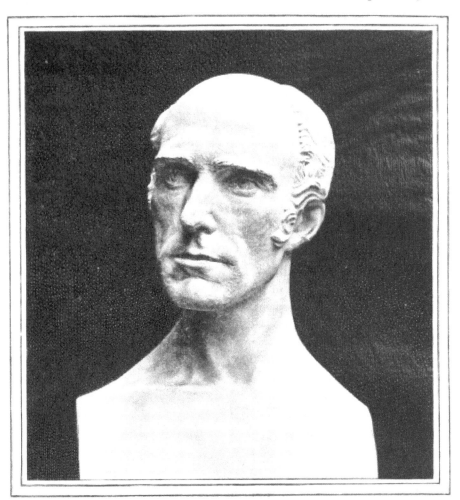

RICHARD RUSH

Age 45

Although Smithson died in 1829, the United States Government was not advised of the gift until six years afterward, when the life estate fell in, and the will was thrown into chancery. It was then that Richard Rush was appointed, by President Jackson, special representative of the government to pursue and secure the property. He was successful, and returned to this country, in August of 1838, with the legacy, amounting to upwards of half a million of dollars. Nothing was done for quite eight years toward carrying into effect the bequest of Smithson, except to ask advice, from eminent scholars and educators, as to the best means of fulfilling the testator's intention. The consensus of opinion was in favor of a university or school for higher education, but Mr. Rush objected to a school of any kind, and proposed a plan which more nearly corresponded, than any other of the early ones, with that which was finally adopted. Thus, both in securing the legacy, and directing the curriculum of the institution, Richard Rush took a most important part.

Mr. Rush's last official service was as minister to France, during the eventful years of 1847 to 1851 and he was the first representative of a foreign power to recognize the new republic. He had a fine literary sense, which he did not fail to cultivate, and his "Narrative of a Residence at the Court of London," and "Washington in Domestic Life," from the papers of Tobias Lear, are standard works. It may not be without interest to add that Mr. Rush was the author of the famous game "Twenty Questions," which has been thought worthy of the consideration of some of the brightest minds in Europe and in America.

XV

EDWIN FORREST

OR many years Edwin Forrest was regarded as the greatest of American tragedians, his nearest rival being his namesake Edwin Booth. Now that the great leveller, death, has claimed them both, it may be questioned if Forrest's supremacy is maintained. The animal was so uppermost in Forrest's nature and person that he was unsuited to the delineation of the finer types of character, and therefore his greatest achievements were in robust parts requiring physical power, where he could rant and rage at will. In youth he must have had a singularly handsome face, and he was but twenty-one, in 1827, when Browere made his life mask. It was during an engagement at the old Bowery theatre, New York, when Forrest was playing "William Tell." It will be observed that the head, which is finely classical, of the Roman type, appears to be bald, while Forrest took great pride in his luxurious locks. This effect happened in this wise. Forrest was a novice on the stage and had just made his first appearance as *William Tell*. Browere saw the performance, and was so struck with the personality of the young actor that he asked permission to take his mask. Forrest consented, but was so afraid the material of the mould might cling to his hair, that he insisted upon wearing a skull-cap during the operation. Some faces change so much from youth to age that it is difficult, if not impossible, to trace any resemblance of the beginning in the end. But the characteristics of feature and expression in Browere's bust of Forrest are also to be found in his latest photographs.

The tragedian was born in old Southwark, Philadelphia, March 9, 1806, and was "stage struck" almost from infancy, playing girl's parts when only twelve years old. In his fifteenth year he made his début at the Walnut Street theatre, Philadelphia, as young *Norval* in the tragedy of "Douglas"; and before he was twenty-one had gained considerable reputation and had played Othello before a New York audience. From this time he enjoyed a vacillating reputation, but was always the stage idol of the masses, while his intense personality kept him from appealing to the refinements of intellect. He died at Philadelphia, December 12, 1872, leaving his fortune, books and paintings to a home for aged actors to be called the Forrest Home; but his estate was largely crippled by claims for unpaid alimony due to his divorced wife, so the home is not exactly what Forrest intended that it should be.

EDWIN FORREST

Age 21

XVI

MARTIN VAN BUREN

THE latest work that we have from the hand of Browere, is the bust from the life mask of "the Little Magician," as Martin Van Buren was called, made in 1833, the year before Browere's death. Van Buren was then in his fifty-first year, and he lived until July 24, 1862. His life covered a longer era and his career witnessed greater changes in national life than those of any other man who has occupied the presidential chair. He was born and died in Kinderhook, Columbia county, New York; studied law with William P. Van Ness, the friend of Burr; and was admitted to the bar on attaining his majority. He was fitted by taste and temperament for politics, and politics were fitted for him.

As early as his eighteenth year, before he had a vote, Van Buren was chosen to take part in a local nominating convention; and as soon as he could act, as well as speak, he became an ardent adherent of the Jeffersonian democracy. His first office was surrogate of his native county, which place he held for five years; and when, in 1811, the proposed recharter of the United States Bank was the leading question of Federal politics, Van Buren took an active part against the measure. The following year he was elected to the Senate of New York, and supported President Madison and the War with England, drawing up the resolution of thanks, voted by the legislature, to General Jackson for his victory at New Orleans.

In 1815, Van Buren became Attorney-General of New York, from which office he was removed four years later, owing to his refusal to adhere to De Witt Clinton, whose policy, excepting as regarded the canal, he did not approve. The politics of New York were in a most feverish and topsy-turvy state, and the many factions could not combine to elect a United States senator in 1818-19, until Van Buren, by his moderation and his genius for political organization, brought about order and harmony, and Rufus King, a political opponent of Van Buren, was chosen to the high office. Two years later Van Buren was rewarded by being also sent to the Senate, and about the same time was chosen delegate to the convention which reviewed the Constitution of New York. In this body he sought to limit the elective franchise to householders, that this invaluable right of citizenship might not be cheapened and the rural districts overborne by the cities. Unfortunately he was in the minority, or such a beneficent provision might have spread over the length and breadth of the land, so that the elective franchise would have retained the value of its high prerogative, and not become the valueless and unwieldy burden that it now is. Van Buren also opposed an elective judiciary, in both of which positions he was in opposition to his own party.

MARTIN VAN BUREN

Age 51

In the United States Senate he was for many years chairman of the Judiciary Committee, and, on the Florida territorial bill voted against the increase of slavery. He was a strict constructionist of the Constitution, recognizing that as the only safe canon of interpretation for a fundamental law; and he had pronounced views in favor of State rights and against the power of the United States Supreme Court, to overthrow State laws, believing this contrary to the provision of the Constitution insuring the inviolability of contracts.

In 1828 he was called from the Senate to the gubernatorial chair of New York, and, supporting Jackson for the Presidency, was made by him Secretary of State, which office he resigned to accept the English mission; but, by the opposition of John C. Calhoun, he was not confirmed. This discreditable action increased Van Buren's popularity, and he succeeded Calhoun as Vice-President for Jackson's second term, soon being regarded as the lineal successor to the Presidency. He was elected, over Harrison and over Webster, pledged to oppose any interference with slavery in the slave States. The ruling act of his administration was one for the lasting benefit of the nation, which never should be forgotten. In his first message to Congress he deprecated the deposit of public moneys in private banks, which had followed Jackson's removal of the deposits from the United States Bank, and urged an independent treasury for the safe-keeping and disbursements of the public money; but it was not until near the close of his administration that he secured congressional assent to the measure. This has been far-reaching in its beneficial effects, and too much honor cannot be accorded Van Buren, for his action in the matter, which has saved the treasury from great financial disruptions. Notwithstanding this, his administration went down in a cloud, and he was overwhelmingly defeated for a second term.

Van Buren was opposed to the extension of slavery, but on all other points was an uncompromising Democrat. On this platform he was again nominated for the Presidency, in 1848, with Charles Francis Adams as Vice-President. The result of his candidature was the defeat of General Cass, the regular Democratic nominee, and the election of General Taylor. After this he retired from public life and devoted his time to the writing of his "Inquiry into the Origin and Course of Political Parties in the United States," a work which has been called more an apology than a history. When the Civil War came upon the nation, Van Buren gave zealous support to the National Government. He was an intense partisan, masterful in leadership, reducing politics to a fine art. It has been well said that, "combining the statesman's foresight with the politician's tact, he showed his sagacity, rather by seeking a majority for his views than by following the views of a majority." He was far from being a demagogue, and he was frequently found fighting on the unpopular side. His convictions were strong, and he adhered to them with tenacity. While from peculiar circumstances his public career has been the subject of much partisan denunciation, he is entitled, both for activity and ability, to a higher niche in the temple of fame than is commonly accorded him. Van Buren was small in stature and of blond coloring. The physiognomist would accord to him penetration, quickness of apprehension and benevolence of disposition, while the phrenologist would add unusual reflective faculties, firmness and caution.

XVII

DEATH MASK OF JAMES MONROE

HE masks that Browere made from the subject in full life, must not be confused in any sense with the more common mask made after death. This confusion could not occur with any one who has had an opportunity to observe Browere's work or to make comparison with the reproductions in this book; but persons not familiar with these portrait busts, and having only some knowledge of masks made after death, or of such life masks as Clark Mills made,—which are thoroughly death-like in their character,—might easily fall into such an error, and, looking upon the latter as repulsive and worthless as portraiture, give no heed to the different character and true value of Browere's living likenesses.

Mr. Laurence Hutton, in his very curious and interesting volume entitled "Portraits in Plaster," says: "The value of a plaster cast as a portrait of the dead or living face cannot for a moment be questioned. It must of necessity be absolutely true to nature. It cannot flatter; it cannot caricature. It shows the subject as he was, not only as others saw him in the actual flesh, but as he saw himself. And in the case of a death mask particularly, it shows the subject often as he permitted no one but himself to see himself. He does not pose; he does not 'try to look pleasant.' In his mask he is seen, as it were, with his mask off."

I do not quote these words, of my accomplished friend Mr. Hutton, simply for the purpose of combating them, but to show how differently two, perfectly sincere, honest delvers after historic truth, can see the same thing. Having made portraiture my study for many years, and thus having in my mind's eye, indelibly fixed, the faces of legions of public men, I have yet to see a death mask that I could recognize at sight; many I could recall when told whose masks they were, but more yet have, to my vision, no resemblance whatever to the living man. Mr. Story, the eminent American sculptor but recently deceased, recognized how untrustworthy even life masks are as portraits. In speaking of what is claimed to be Houdon's original mask of Washington, which Mr. Story owned, he wrote: "Indeed, a mask from the living face, though it repeats exactly the true forms of the original, lacks the spirit and expression of the real person." So true is this, that when Mr. St. Gaudens first saw Clark Mills's life mask of President Lincoln, he insisted that it was a death mask; for, without "the spirit and expression," where can the likeness be? As Sir Joshua Reynolds says in one of his Discourses: "In portraits, the grace and, we may add, the likeness consists more in taking the general air than in observing the exact similitude of every feature." In photography we have "the exact similitude of every feature," yet how often are photographs bad likenesses, because they lack "the spirit and expression"!

While it is possible to preserve "the spirit and expression" as well as to give "the exact similitude of every feature" in a life mask, as exemplified in the marvellous work of Browere, it is impossible in a death mask, for these evanescent qualities are then gone. I am not quite certain that even "the exact similitude of every feature" is preserved in a death mask; certainly the natural relation of one feature to another is not. The death mask may, to a degree, be a correct reproduction of the bony structure, but only to a limited degree as it was in nature, for the obvious reason that the ligaments, holding the sections of bone together in their proper places, become relaxed with dissolution, and the bones lose their exact positions, which condition even the slight weight of the plaster increases.

Masks, too, will sometimes approach caricature, if they will not flatter, for they will reproduce peculiarities of formation which may not be observable superficially. This view is emphasized by Lavater in his "Physiognomy," as quoted by Mr. Hutton. Lavater writes: "The dead and the impressions of the dead, taken in plaster, are not less worthy of observation [than the living faces]. The settled features *are much more prominent* than in the living and in the sleeping. What life makes fugitive, death arrests. What was undefinable, is defined. All is reduced to its proper level; each trait is in its exact proportion, unless excruciating disease or accident have preceded death." This is undoubtedly true from the point of view of the physiognomist, and it is his much desired vantage-ground, for his only object is to read the features laid bare.

From Browere's hand we have but one death mask, and although it is open to much of the objection urged against death masks generally, it is superior to any other death mask I have ever seen. It is difficult to believe it was made after life was gone, so vibrant with life it seems. It possesses more living, breathing qualities than the life masks made by other men. If any proof were needed of the inestimable value of Browere's lost process for making masks, it can be found in the quality of this death mask of James Monroe.

Monroe's name is perhaps more familiarly known to the public than that of any other President, save Washington and Lincoln, owing to its association with the doctrine, which he promulgated, of non-interference on the western hemisphere by European nations, known as the "Monroe Doctrine." He was the fourth of the seven Virginian Presidents, and left William and Mary College, when only eighteen, as a lieutenant in Hugh Mercer's regiment, to join Washington's army. He served throughout the Revolutionary War, having been wounded at Trenton, and was present at Monmouth, Brandywine, and Germantown. In 1782 he took his seat in the Assembly of Virginia, and later was a delegate to Congress. Monroe took an active part in the controversy relative to the settlement of the Northwest Territory, which was quieted only by the Ordinance of 1787; and although he had a hand in originating the convention to frame a constitution for the General Government, he was not a member of it, and opposed the ratification of its work.

DEATH MASK OF JAMES MONROE

He was elected to the Senate of the United States in 1790, and held the office until he was sent as minister to France, four years later. He was a bitter anti-Federalist and opponent of the administration of Washington, so that his appointment to France came as a great surprise; and his action in recognizing the Republic, was an even greater surprise to his home government. For this he was reprimanded, and on his return published a defence of his conduct. He was Governor of Virginia, from 1797 to 1802, and returned to France as special envoy to negotiate with Napoleon the purchase of Louisiana. He was again Governor of Virginia, but resigned to accept the portfolio of state in Madison's cabinet, which was the stepping-stone to the succession in the Presidency. This high office he held for two terms, and for the last term there was only one electoral vote cast against him. It was in the second year of his second term, 1823, that he enunciated the famous Monroe Doctrine of "Hands off!" contained in two brief paragraphs in his annual message, which doctrine is logically nullified by the present foreign policy of the country.

Monroe's administration has been designated "the Era of Good Feeling," and he should always be remembered as an upright and honest politician. As is too often the case with men who give their best years to the public service, his latter days were burdened by intense poverty, and he died in New York, July 4, 1831, almost in want.

In person Monroe was tall, well formed, and with a fair complexion and blue eyes. The well-known portraits of him, by Stuart and by Vanderlyn, tail to bestow any signs of recognition upon Browere's death mask; but it is true these two portraits were painted a score and more years before Monroe's death. While, as has been said, it is far more life-like than many life casts, its reproduction only serves to emphasize my views as to the little value of death masks as portraits.

ADDENDUM TO CHAPTER VIII

Since this chapter went to press there has been published Roland's "Life of Charles Carroll of Carrollton," and upon page 342, of Volume II, there appears the following letter from Charles Carroll, upon his bust, by Browere, which is too important not to be given a place here:

DOUGHOREGAN MANOR, July 29, 1826.

Sir:

Mr. Browere has produced and read to me several letters from sundry most respectable personages; on their recommendation and at his request I sat to him to take my bust. He has taken it, and in my opinion and that of my family, and of all who have seen it, the resemblance is most striking. The operation from its commencement to its completion was performed in two hours, with very little inconvenience and no pain to myself. This bust Mr. Browere contemplates placing, with many others, in a national gallery of busts. That his efforts may be crowned with success is my earnest wish. That his talents and genius deserve it I have no hesitation in pronouncing. I remain, with great respect, Sir, your most humble servant

CH. CARROLL OF CARROLLTON.

To ARCHIBALD ROBERTSON, ESQ.

In "Niles's Register" for August 12, 1826, (Volume XXX, page 411,) is given an account of this bust and its public exhibition at the Exchange in Baltimore.

INDEX

Lector House believes that a society develops through a two-fold approach of continuous learning and adaptation, which is derived from the study of classic literary works spread across the historic timeline of literature records. Therefore, we aim at reviving, repairing and redeveloping all those inaccessible or damaged but historically as well as culturally important literature across subjects so that the future generations may have an opportunity to study and learn from past works to embark upon a journey of creating a better future.

This book is a result of an effort made by Lector House towards making a contribution to the preservation and repair of original ancient works which might hold historical significance to the approach of continuous learning across subjects.

HAPPY READING & LEARNING!

LECTOR HOUSE
LECTOR HOUSE LLP
E-MAIL: lectorpublishing@gmail.com

CPSIA information can be obtained
at www.ICGtesting.com
Printed in the USA
BVHW040849130822
644445BV00018B/374